Creative Book Reports
Fun Projects with Rubrics
for Fiction and Nonfiction

Jane Feber

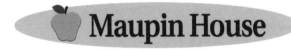

D1472844

Creative Book Reports:
Fun Projects with Rubrics for Fiction and Nonfiction

Cover Design: Gaye Dell
Photography and Layout: Digital Photo, Inc.

Library of Congress Cataloging-in-Publication Data

Feber, Jane, 1951-
    Creative book reports : fun projects with rubrics for fiction and
nonfoiction / by Jane Feber.-- 1st ed.
        p. cm.
    Includes index.
    ISBN 0-929895-69-X
  1.   Literature--Study and teaching (Elementary)--Activity programs. 2.
Literature--Study and teaching (Middle school)--Activity programs. 3.
Language arts (Elementary) --Activity programs. 4.   Language arts (Middle
school)--Activity programs. I. Title.
    LB1575.F43 2004
    372.64--dc22
                                            2004001564

Maupin House publishes professional resources that improve student performance. Inquire about scheduling on-site training, author visits, or about ordering resources.

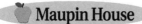

Maupin House Publishing
PO Box 90148
Gainesville, FL 32607
800-524-0634 / 352-373-5588
352-373-5546 (fax)
www.maupinhouse.com / info@maupinhouse.com

10 9 8 7 6 5 4 3 2 1

Dedication

I dedicate this book to my husband, Dan, for his patience while I worked day and night, weekends and vacations; and to my dear friend, Linda Bishop, who shared my projects with her students and her students' enthusiasm for the projects with me.

Contents

Contents

Introduction

Why Alternative Responses to Literature?

For a long time, we teachers have depended on the traditional, paper book report to judge whether or not our students really understand the literary elements of fiction. But today's upper elementary classroom is a far more complex place than ever before. Students must work toward specific objectives and satisfy state-mandated performance standards, not only in language arts but also for social studies and science as well.

While the traditional book report focused mainly on responding to fiction, it's not terribly well-suited for informational genres. How can we include responses to nonfiction literature and content-area topics and subjects that now appear on state assessments (and which students also enjoy reading!)?

Creative Book Reports gives you 39 hands-on projects that help your students expand their book report horizons. These alternative responses to literature will engage your students as they demonstrate their knowledge of literary elements such as plot, character, setting, and theme in fiction – or their comprehension of informational selections or content-area concepts.

The alternative response ideas in this resource go well beyond the very narrow scope of the traditional—and much overused—book report, and also satisfy our need to ensure that students are working to performance standards. Alternative responses to literature allow students freedom of expression. They provide a concrete and visual way for each student to explore literature response. And they give us teachers an alternative assessment option.

All of the projects in this resource help students to synthesize information of large concepts into smaller pieces in visual and concrete ways. They provide opportunities for students to work in various media, thus better meeting the needs of the visual, the kinesthetic, and the auditory learner. And instead of tending to point to one "correct" answer, alternative responses to literature encourage critical and creative thinking.

Best of all, the learning "sticks." Because these projects actively engage students, learning becomes fun. As writer Alfred Mercier once said, "What we learn with pleasure, we never forget."

Why Use Rubrics?

When students know what's expected of them, the quality of their responses increases. Each project in this book comes with a rubric of clearly stated objectives, which research has shown to positively affect student achievement. (Wise, Kevin & Okey, James. *Journal of Research in Science Teaching*. pp 419 – 435, 1983).

Rubrics appeal to teachers and students alike. Rubrics give students a working guide that clearly spells out the criteria on which their work will be evaluated before they begin their projects. Students use the rubrics to focus their efforts. They can easily see what areas of their work need improvement. The objective, justifiable standards on the rubrics also make it easier for teachers to assess that work, too.

The grading rubric attached to each student project allows you to assess student performance on individual parts of the project. For example, while one student may immediately grasp the idea of the importance of plot, he or she might not be able to fully comprehend setting. Using a rubric allows students with varying abilities and learning styles to become successful because you, the teacher, are able to provide assistance with objectives with which a student may have difficulty. Later, these rubrics also can be used in parent conferences or to assess improvement throughout the school year.

The rubrics in this resource attach point values to each of the assessment criteria in an assigned project. Each criterion is listed individually on the student reproducible page. Some rubrics are based on a 50-point scale, but the point breakdowns can easily be doubled to increase a project's value to 100.

For your convenience, the rubrics also can be found on the CD, formatted in Microsoft Word®. This makes it easy to adapt them to fit specific subject-area needs, or alter to focus on specific performance goals, such as response length or number of paragraphs you will require. The rubrics are as adaptable and flexible as you need them to be.

When you use rubrics to grade, assessment is made easy. When I use rubrics, for example, I circle any objectives that are missing and determine the points awarded. When assessing the grammar and punctuation, I simply put a slash mark on the rubric for each miscue. This way, I can quickly compute the total points awarded and have time left to attach a "Good Work" sticker to the rubric, or to write an instructional note for the student. All the grading criteria are stated clearly so that projects can be rapidly and objectively graded.

How to Use this Book

Variety is truly the spice of life—especially when talking about literature response! The many different kinds of book report projects in this resource will keep your students excited about learning over the entire year.

Most projects described are designed as a response to a single book that would be read and shared by the entire class, but every project can be adapted for separate books which are assigned to small groups or for independent reading. Most can be done either in class or assigned as homework. They are versatile enough to fit into social studies or science lesson plans, too. And because you can teach many different concepts with the same project, you will find you'll save lesson-preparation time as well.

The Project Page Format on page xi shows you where the information for each lesson is located. Read that first to become familiar with the format.

Note that projects are organized by presentation media. Those projects listed with subtitles include rubrics that are specific to those projects. Rubrics for projects without subtitles should be changed to fit the book or topic you want to assess.

Of course, every one of the projects can be adapted for your needs. "Other Ideas" are listed for every project, with suggestions for applying it for language arts, science, or social studies. There's also a cross-index at the back of the book to help you organize the projects by content or topic.

Try all of the projects at least once and see what works for you and your students. When focusing on one performance standard, it is possible to have each class work on a different project. Where one class is making character cards, another could be preparing character cutouts. This gives you a chance to see what works best for your teaching situation, to make instructional adjustments according to your classroom needs, and to have fun facilitating while your students are actively engaged in responding to literature.

Classroom Management Tips

As most teachers realize, time spent on a task varies from group to group. Many of the projects in this book could be completed in one or two class periods, but since most teachers don't focus solely on literature for that length of time, I suggest planning 20- to 30-minute blocks of time for several class periods until the project is complete.

Start preparing by collecting the materials needed for the presentation you will use. The materials needed for each project will be listed on every Teacher Page. Keep your project materials organized, labeled, and stored in the classroom for easy access. Make a project yourself before you introduce it to students to make it easier to explain.

Prepare your rubrics according to your book, topic, or theme. Choose a presentation method that you like and adapt the rubric to fit, or use a project that already lists an application. You can change the rubrics as you like with the CD, or use them as is from the reproducible pages.

When you introduce a project for the first time, construct a model or have one available for the students to see and handle as you explain it. From that point on, keep one or two of your students' projects to show as examples for the next class.

On the first day of the project, give students their reproducible pages with the directions and rubrics and allow them time to brainstorm, conference with one another (if necessary), and write a rough draft that reflects the project's performance standards. When the students have completed their projects, they will turn in their reproducible pages (with their names clearly written on them!) in order to receive their grades.

On the first day of a multi-day project, give them time to organize their ideas on paper as a rough draft. The second day is a good time for peer review. Allow students time to share their drafts with each other and provide constructive criticism. (I ask students to paste sticky notes on their friends' papers with comments for revision.) The remaining time during this class period is used for revision. If the project requires research, I usually set aside two or three 30-minute periods in the school media center. The following day or two, I allow students to transfer their revised work to complete their final projects.

Students should be allowed to interact when they work on projects, and some projects in this resource are specifically designed for group work. Group work is a useful activity for teaching real-world situations. Knowing that they will be graded on how well they function within a group dynamic will help your students to sharpen their interpersonal skills.

Quite often, task talk is good talk. Walk around the classroom while students are working; listen to what they are saying and interject your ideas. Conversation builds good group dynamics, and it's your job to facilitate.

Typed work on a final project is always preferred. It not only looks nicer, it's easier to read. Require it if you can, but for students who don't have access to a computer, ask them to print neatly. For those students who have a computer at home, drafts can be revised in class, prepared at home, and attached to the projects when they return to school.

How to Display Projects

With limited bulletin board and wall space in a classroom, a creative solution for display of student projects is essential. One solution that works in my classroom is a clothesline running between the walls at the back of the class. This line stretches from one side of the room to the other. I purchased a roll of wire and two eye hooks that the school custodian placed in the walls. Using clothespins, I am able to display flipbooks, envelopes, mini-books, character cutouts, and many other projects.

If a permanent clothesline is not possible in your classroom, look for a place to run a string or wire from cabinet to cabinet. Hang mobiles from the ceiling with paper clips that fit between the ceiling tiles. Bulletin boards or display cases in the hallway or cafeteria are also great places for students to view each other's work, and don't forget that the media center will gladly welcome student projects, especially those that focus on literature.

No matter how or where the work is exhibited, you'll find that students love seeing their "published" works on display. They will enjoy reading—and getting ideas from—other students' presentations for their next project.

Project Page Format

Student Page

Teacher Page

A quick introduction to the project.

Project description: Includes a project description and explanation. Projects without subtitles supply the presentation idea, and the rubric also is non-specific. The rubrics with projects with subtitles describe one specific use for the project.

A space for the student's name. Students turn in this rubric page with their projects.

Materials: Lists materials needed for each student.

Every student page will begin with a quick introduction.

Accordion Book

NAME_____

Your task is to present information in a simple six-section booklet. You will need a file folder to complete this project.

Directions:

1. You will need one file folder to make the accordion book. Lay the file flat and cut off the irregular edge on either side (if necessary).
2. Cut it in half along the crease.
3. Connect the two halves by taping the short ends together.
4. Starting at one short end, fold every 3" backwards and forwards like an accordion. You should now have six equal sections.
5. The cover section should include an appropriate title and illustration for the topic being studied. The six sections inside should each include information on
6. Write your name on the back of the last section.

Rubric for Accordion Book:

_____cover is titled and illustrated; name is on the back panel (8 points)

_____section one is described well; illustrated (10 points)

_____section two is described well; illustrated (10 points)

_____section three is described well; illustrated (10 points)

_____section four is described well; illustrated (10 points)

_____section five is described well; illustrated (10 points)

_____section six is described well; illustrated (10 points)

_____correct use of grammar, spelling, punctuation, capitalization, and complete sentences (22 points)

_____neat/attractive appearance (10 points)

_____FINAL GRADE/100

Accordion Book

Teacher Page

This easy-to-make booklet allows students to break down complicated units of study into a handful of simple parts.

Project Description: Using this versatile presentation method, students construct a six-section accordion book to display information on a given topic.

Materials:
_____ one file folder per student   _____cellophane tape
_____ markers, crayons, and/or colored pencils

Suggestions:
Depending on the topic being studied, students may need three or four class periods in order to research their topic in the school's media center.
If computers are available, students might also be able to use the Internet for research sources and/or illustrations.

Other Ideas:
Language Arts - literary elements (sections can be labeled character, setting, plot, conflict/resolution, and theme); a poetry unit (students will select a poem, write it in one section and use the following sections to provide an illustration, a written interpretation, and various examples of literary devices—metaphors, similes, alliteration, onomatopoeia, etc.)

Science - the body's systems, simple machines, animals, plants, or ecosystems

Social Studies - countries, bodies of water, wars, famous people, laws, or geographical terms

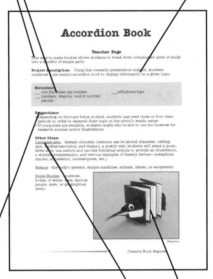

Creative Book Reports

Directions: Step-by-step directions

Suggestions: Includes how-to tips to prepare and present the project.

Rubric: The rubric assigns points for each part of the project, with a total at the bottom. Use the reproducible in the book, or create your own from the rubrics on the CD, which are formatted in Word. Rubrics can be tailored to fit specific books or project needs across the curriculum. Note that the rubrics for projects listed without a subtitle are non-specific. Rubrics for projects with a subtitle contain specific directions for that project.

Other Ideas: Suggestions for adapting projects for language arts, history, social studies, and science.

Photograph: Included for many of the projects.

Accordion Book

NAME_____

Your task is to present information in a simple six-section booklet. You will need a file folder to complete this project.

Directions:

1. You will need one file folder to make the accordion book. Lay the file flat and cut off the irregular edges on either side (if necessary).
2. Cut it in half along the crease.
3. Connect the two halves by taping the short ends together.
4. Starting at one short end, fold every 5" backwards and forwards like an accordion. You should now have six equal sections.
5. The cover section should include an appropriate title and illustration for the topic being studied. Each of the six sections should include information on the topic and an appropriate illustration.
6. Write your name on the back of the last section.

Rubric for Accordion Book:

_____cover is titled and illustrated; name is on the back panel (5 points)

_____section one is described well; illustrated (10 points)

_____section two is described well; illustrated (10 points)

_____section three is described well; illustrated (10 points)

_____section four is described well; illustrated (10 points)

_____section five is described well; illustrated (10 points)

_____section six is described well; illustrated (10 points)

_____correct use of grammar, spelling, punctuation, capitalization, and complete sentences (25 points)

_____neat/attractive appearance (10 points)

_____FINAL GRADE/100

Accordion Book

Teacher Page

This easy-to-make booklet allows students to break down complicated units of study into a handful of simple parts.

Project Description: Using this versatile presentation method, students construct a six-section accordion book to display information on a given topic.

Materials:
___ one file folder per student   ___cellophane tape
___ markers, crayons, and/or colored
    pencils

Suggestions:
- Depending on the topic being studied, students may need three or four class periods in order to research their topic in the school's media center.
- If computers are available, students might also be able to use the Internet for research sources and/or illustrations.

Other Ideas:

Language Arts - literary elements (sections can be labeled character, setting, plot, conflict/resolution, and theme); a poetry unit (students will select a poem, write it on one section and use the following sections to provide an illustration, a written interpretation, and various examples of literary devices—metaphors, similes, alliteration, onomatopoeia, etc.)

Science - the body's systems, simple machines, animals, plants, or ecosystems

Social Studies - countries, bodies of water, wars, famous people, laws, or geographical terms

Penguins

Audiotape
Audio Advertisement

NAME_____

Your task is to create an ad for a book you have read. Noise effects or character voices can add fun and variety to your advertisement. Make sure not to give away the ending!

Directions:

1. Write a script advertising a book you have read. Make sure to mention the author and title in the beginning of the script. You could begin with a statement such as, "You've got to read (title) by (author's name)."
2. Use persuasive techniques to entice others to read this piece. Some hints: describe the plot without telling the ending and mention a major conflict without telling its resolution. You could also describe characters' behaviors to make the listeners want to get to know these characters better.
3. At the end of your script there should be a strong persuasive statement that makes the listener want to read this story or novel.
4. You will read the script into the tape recorder. It should be about 3-5 minutes long. Remember to speak slowly, clearly, and loudly enough for your audience to hear.
5. Turn in your script when you're done. Make sure your name is written on it. You will play the tape for the class.

Rubric for Audio Advertisement:

_____audiotape begins with a positive statement about the book using the title and author (5 points)

_____plot is described without telling the ending (15 points)

_____a major conflict in the story is mentioned; resolution is not provided (15 points)

_____the description of characters' behaviors make listeners want to know these characters better (15 points)

_____strong closing makes listeners want to read this book (5 points)

_____persuasive techniques entice others to read this genre of literature (5 points)

_____script is written using correct grammar, spelling, punctuation, capitalization, and complete sentences (15 points)

_____audio is clear; student speaks slowly and loudly enough for the class to hear; stayed within the 3-5 minute time limit (25 points)

_____FINAL GRADE/100

Audiotape
Audio Advertisement

Teacher Page

All children are familiar with commercials on TV and radio, so this one should be fun and easy for them to do. You could encourage them to model their advertisement after one of their favorites.

Project Description: Students will write and record an advertisement encouraging classmates to read a short story, novel, or informational text.

Materials:
___paper
___pen or pencil
___audio tape
___tape recorder

Suggestions:
• Before you begin this project, go over what a good speaking voice sounds like (loud, clear, speak slowly) and also emphasize the traits of a persuasive argument (engage the listener and move them to action).
• You could record a few radio commercials and play them for your students in class. This modeling process may help them imagine what their own advertisement will sound like.
• Encourage students to use sound effects: running water for the ocean or river, a fan for wind, wooden blocks hit together for a horse's hooves, even brothers and sisters in the background to create various effects work well. You'll be surprised at how creative your students can be!
• If students want to work in groups, everyone in the group should help write the script and be included in the recording.
• Students could also write a script that discourages their classmates from reading a specific short story or novel.
• Allow students time to rehearse their presentations.

Other Ideas:
Language Arts - Students can choose a chapter from a novel or a short story and record themselves as they explain the literary elements present in their selection: character, setting, plot, conflict, resolution, and theme.

Nonfiction - Students can record themselves explaining the five 'Ws' of any informational piece: who, what, when, where, and why.

Award
And the Winner Is...

NAME_____

Your task is to perform an award ceremony for an important figure. You'll write a short speech and create an award to present in class.

Directions:

1. Pick an important person from your unit of study, consider his or her accomplishments, and determine an appropriate award for those accomplishments.
2. Prepare a speech (maximum three minutes) about the person. Tell why you chose this person and describe his or her accomplishments. Explain the reasons you chose to present this particular award to this person.
3. Design an award for this person. For example, you could present Alexander Graham Bell a replica of a telephone. Awards can also be as simple as a certificate. Either way, be creative!
4. The award must include (in writing) the person's name and accomplishment(s). Write your name on the back of the award.
5. Present the award in class. Make sure to keep eye contact with your audience and speak slowly and clearly. Presentation should be no more than three minutes long. You may ask a partner to dress up as the person and accept the award.

Rubric for And the Winner Is...:

_____speech highlights person's accomplishments (15 points)

_____speech is written using correct grammar, punctuation, spelling, and complete sentences (10 points)

_____award includes the person's name and accomplishments (5 points)

_____award is neat/attractive (5 points)

_____evidence that the speech was well-rehearsed: either plenty of eye contact OR you are dressed in character (10 points)

_____your name is on the back of the award (5 points)

_____FINAL GRADE/50

Award
And the Winner Is...

Teacher Page

Whether it's a "Great Job!" sticker or a certificate of achievement, students love giving and receiving awards. This project works well as a solo project or when done in pairs.

Project Description: Students will choose one person from a unit of study and prepare an award and speech to celebrate the person's accomplishments.

Materials:
(vary depending on award given)
___construction paper
___markers, crayons, and/or colored pencils
(Also see Suggestions)

Suggestions:
• Encourage students to be creative with the awards they construct. For example, James Audubon could be presented with a birdhouse or Alexander Graham Bell, a replica of a telephone.
• Students may read their speech and ask another student to come up to receive the award. Or you can read the student's speech and present the award to the student dressed in character.
• Awards can also be as simple as a certificate; just make sure the award includes the person's name and his or her accomplishments.
• Allow students time to rehearse their presentations.

Other Ideas:
Language Arts - fictional characters

History - inventors, great leaders, war heroes, scientists

Bifold Booklet
Conflict/Resolution Bifold

NAME_____

Your task is to construct a bifold out of a piece of paper in order to illustrate and explain conflict and resolution in a short story or novel.

Directions:

1. Fold a sheet of 8 1/2" x 11" paper in half from top to bottom, crease.
2. Fold it in half again from left to right. Unfold and lay flat.
3. Next, cut the paper on the vertical crease from the bottom to the center fold.
4. Fold in half, and position the paper so that the cut side is at the top. This creates the bifold.
5. Write the title of the story at the top of the left flap. Write the author's name at the top of the right-side flap.
6. On the left-side flap, describe a major conflict from this story. Write the word "Conflict" at the bottom of the flap. Illustrate.
7. On the inside left panel, describe the resolution to this conflict. Label this panel "Resolution." Illustrate.
8. Repeat steps 6 and 7 on the right side of the bifold, choosing another conflict and resolution from the story.
9. Write your name on the back side of the bifold.

Rubric for Conflict/Resolution Bifold:

_____title and author are written across the top of the front two flaps (5 points)

_____a conflict in the story is well-described on the front left flap (15 points)

_____a resolution to this conflict is well-described on the inside of the left panel (15 points)

_____a conflict in the story is well-described on the front right flap (15 points)

_____a resolution to this conflict is well-described on the inside right panel (15 points)

_____illustrations are provided for both conflicts and resolutions (10 points)

_____correct use of grammar, punctuation, spelling, capitalization, and complete sentences (20 points)

_____your name appears on the back side of the bifold (5 points)

_____FINAL GRADE/100

Bifold Booklet
Conflict/Resolution Bifold

Teacher Page

This project works well to represent the relationship between conflict and resolution in an understandable, visual way. It can also be used in all subjects to define terms and concepts.

Project Description: Students will select two conflicts in a short story or novel and construct a bifold that illustrates the conflicts and their resolutions. Projects can be adapted to contrast historical figures and events or scientific concepts.

Materials:
___8 1/2" x 11" paper   ___scissors
___markers, crayons, and/or colored
   pencils

Suggestions:
Use this project in all subjects and see what works best for you.

Other Ideas:
Language Arts - Settings—Students can select two settings from a short story or novel read. On the two front flaps, students will write "Setting 1" and "Setting 2." Underneath the flaps, students will describe and illustrate the settings. Figurative language—Students can label the two front flaps with literary devices such as simile, personification, imagery, metaphor, onomatopoeia, etc. Underneath, students will provide an example from the story or poem read, an interpretation, and an illustration.

Science - Students can label their two front flaps "Vertebrates" and "Invertebrates" and describe and illustrate them underneath. For plants, "Monocot" and "Dicot" or "Chemical Properties" and "Physical Properties" can be used.

Social Studies - Students can label the two front flaps "Northern colonies" and "Southern colonies" and compare similarities and differences. They can also use the bifold to describe two people from a given time period.

Brochure
American Revolution Brochure

NAME_____

Your task is to construct a five-panel brochure that describes and illustrates a colony's part in the American Revolutionary War.

Directions:

1. Fold a piece of 8 $^{1/2}$ " x 11" paper into three equal sections from one short end to the other—fold the right third towards the center and the left third towards the center so it overlaps the right.
2. On the outside panel, title your brochure "The American Revolution: (colony name)."
3. As you open up the brochure, title the first section (on the left), "A Visit to (colony name)." Describe this colony and illustrate.
4. Title the second segment "The Role (colony name) Played in the War Effort." Describe this colony's role and illustrate.
5. Section three (the center panel) will be titled "Battles that Took Place in (colony name)." Describe a battle or battles that took place in this colony. Illustrate.
6. The final section (the inside right panel) will be titled "An Important Leader in (colony name)." Describe this leader and provide an illustration.
7. Write your name on the back of your brochure.

Rubric for American Revolution Brochure:

_____front of brochure has title including the colony you chose; illustrated (5 points)

_____section one provides a well-described vision of this colony; illustrated (15 points)

_____section two describes the role this colony played in the war effort; illustrated (15 points)

_____section three describes a battle(s) that took place in this colony; illustrated (15 points)

_____section four describes a leader in this colony and his/her accomplishments; illustrated (15 points)

_____correct use of grammar, spelling, punctuation, capitalization, complete sentences (20 points)

_____neat/attractive appearance (10 points)

_____your name is on the back of the brochure (5 points)

_____FINAL GRADE/100

Brochure
American Revolution Brochure

Teacher Page

Much less intimidating than a full-length report, a five-part brochure allows students to break down larger concepts into smaller pieces.

Project Description: After learning about the American Revolution from either a fictional or nonfictional text, students will prepare a brochure describing a colony involved in the war effort.

Materials:
___ 8 1/2" x 11" paper

___ markers, crayons, and/or colored pencils

Suggestions:
- Give students time in the media center to research the colony they choose. (Three class periods should be adequate time for students to gather information.)
- You can give or suggest titles for each panel of the brochure, such as "A Visit to (colony name)" for the first inside panel.
- Illustrations can be drawn or copied and pasted in the brochure.
- Combine this format with whatever concept you're teaching, from grammar and punctuation to thematic units.

Other Ideas:

<u>Language arts</u> - To describe a character or provide a plot summary. You can also assign one literary element per section (character, setting, plot, conflict, and resolution).

<u>Science</u> - To provide information (organized into five parts) on plants, animals, elements, or a human body system.

<u>Social Studies</u> - To produce a travel brochure for a city, state, or country.

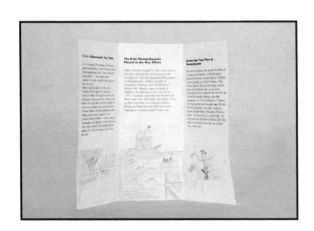

Business Card
Here's My Card

Your task is to create a business card for a character in a short story or novel. Pick a profession that you feel would suit the character you chose based his/her personality and actions.

Directions:

1. Select a character to create a business card for. Pick one that you feel exhibits the characteristics needed for a certain job or service.
2. After learning about different business card formats, create a business card for your character that includes a company name or slogan, the character's name and job title, address, phone number, and email. Include a small illustration.
3. On the back side of the business card, explain why you selected this particular job or service for this character, using facts and information about the character that you learned from the story.
4. Write your name on the back of the business card.

Rubric for Here's My Card:

_____card includes character's name, service provided or slogan advertising a service, address, phone number, and e-mail address (15 points)

_____paragraph on reverse side includes information about the character's personality, interests, and behaviors (15 points)

_____correct use of grammar, spelling, punctuation, capitalization, and complete sentences (10 points)

_____card is illustrated; neatly presented (5 points)

_____your name is on the back of the card (5 points)

_____FINAL GRADE/50

Business Card
Here's My Card

Teacher Page

Succinct and straightforward, this format allows your students to condense important information about a character into a concise business-card format.

Project Description: After completing a short story or novel, students will create a realistic business card advertising a job or service the character could perform based on the qualities and attributes the character displays in the short story or novel.

Materials:
___ 3" x 5" index cards
___ markers and/or colored pencils
___ stickers (optional)

Suggestions:
- Before you begin this lesson, you should show a number of business cards to the class. Students can bring in and pass around business cards from their parents to look at different layouts. Save these from year to year for models. Point out the specific contact information and any images or slogans that help to personalize the card or identify the card's owner.
- Students with computer access and knowledge could prepare their final business cards on a computer.

Other Ideas:
Science - inventors, scientists

Social Studies - explorers, war heroes, great leaders, sports figures

Can
Canning a Character

NAME_____

Your task is to create a doll in the likeness of a character from the short story, novel, or informational text you have read, then place it in a can container.

Directions:

1. Select a character you want to "can."
2. Write a brief sketch of that character on a piece of paper small enough to fit on the container you chose for the assignment. Make sure you include physical characteristics, personality traits, and the character's behavior in the piece you read. Don't forget to proofread!
3. Next, create a doll in the likeness of your character. You may use a doll you already have or make one out of any materials you have handy: stockings stuffed with cotton, Styrofoam balls and popsicle sticks, etc.
4. Make sure you add enough details (hair color, clothes, accessories, etc.) so that the doll can be recognized as your character. Be creative!
5. Place your character inside the container you chose (can, bag, box, basket, etc.).
6. Paste your character sketch on the container and label it with the title of the piece you read, the author, and the character's name.
7. Write your name on the other side of the container.

Rubric for Canning a Character:

_____ title, author, and character's name are visible on outside of container (5 points)

_____ written description includes character's physical attributes, behavior, thoughts, feelings, personality, and what others think of the character (30 points)

_____ character likeness is three-dimensional; character likeness and written description show similar characteristics (25 points)

_____ use of correct grammar, spelling, punctuation, capitalization, and complete sentences (25 points)

_____ neat/attractive presentation (10 points)

_____ your name is visible (5 points)

_____ FINAL GRADE/100 points

Can
Canning a Character

Teacher Page

Teach your students the many and varied elements of characterization by having them design and "can" a likeness of a character in a short story or novel.

Project Description: After completing a short story, novel, or nonfiction work, students will write a brief sketch of the character, create a doll in the likeness of the character, and present it in a can with the sketch glued to it.

Materials:
___ a doll or materials to construct a doll (Styrofoam balls, popsicle sticks, yarn for hair, wallpaper or fabric for clothes, etc.)

___ a container (can, bag, box, basket)
___ notebook or construction paper
___ pencil or pen
___ glue

Suggestions:
- Have students bring "junk" suitable for doll-making from home. Encourage them to share their materials when constructing their characters.
- Dolls' bodies can be made from plastic bottles cut up the middle for legs, stockings stuffed with cotton, a Styrofoam ball for a head with popsicle sticks for arms and legs, cardboard cut-outs, etc.
- Encourage your students to add details and accessories to better reflect the character's personality, hobbies, interests, and role in the short story or novel (features can be made from beads, buttons, yarn, crayons, etc.; clothes can be paper, wallpaper, felt, or fabric).
- For nonfiction, allow students time to research their person in the media center before starting the project. Have students include the person's photo, birth/death dates, accomplishments, and the impact he or she had on the student's life.

Other Ideas:
Science - famous inventors or scientists

Social Studies - great leaders, sports figures, war heroes, explorers

CDs
Literary Elements CD

NAME_____

In this project you will design five CDs—both front and back—that illustrate the five literary elements in a short story or novel.

Directions:

1. Use the cardboard CD cutout as a template to cut out 5 circles the size of a CD. The circle must have a hole in the center to fit in a CD case.
2. Label the first CD "Character." Describe a character in the story on one side. Draw an illustration that represents that character on the opposite side.
3. The second CD will be labeled "Setting." On this CD, describe a setting from the story and draw an illustration on the opposite side.
4. The third CD will be labeled "Conflict" on one side and "Resolution" on the other. Write about a specific conflict on one side and provide an illustration. On the other side, explain the resolution and provide an illustration.
5. The fourth CD will be labeled "Plot" and will consist of a description of the major events of the story on one side and an illustration on the other.
6. The final CD will be labeled "Theme." On one side, describe a theme that runs throughout the story and illustrate the theme on the other side.
7. Provide the title and author of the story and an illustration on the cover of the case. You can do this on a sheet of white drawing paper cut to fit the outside of the case and paste it on. Place the CDs inside the CD case.
8. Write your name on the back of the case.

Rubric for Comprehension CDs:

_____front of CD case has title, author, illustration; your name is on the back (5 points)

_____Character CD description includes character's physical attributes, personality, behavior, thoughts and feelings; illustrated and labeled (15 points)

_____Setting CD describes setting with vivid vocabulary; illustrated and labeled (15 points)

_____Conflict/Resolution described; CD illustrated and labeled "Conflict" on one side and "Resolution" on the other (15 points)

_____Plot CD describes important events that occur; illustrated and labeled (15 points)

_____theme is clearly stated; CD illustrated and labeled "Theme" (15 points)

_____correct spelling, usage, punctuation, capitalization, complete sentences; neatly presented (20 points)

_____FINAL GRADE/100

CDs
Literary Elements CD

Teacher Page

Most students are familiar with CDs and many will have CD cases they can bring in for this project.

Project Description: Students will design a CD case and five CDs to describe the literary elements of a short story, novel, or informational text.

Materials:
___ empty CD cases (have students bring them in)
___ cardboard circles the size of CDs
___ white construction paper
___ markers, crayons, and/or colored pencils
___ scissors
___ glue
___ notebook
___ pens

Suggestions:
• Remind the students to carefully locate the hole in the center of the CD so it will fit in the CD case. It's a good idea to pass several blank CDs around the class for students to trace.
• This adapts well for any literary element, such as plot, setting, or conflict/resolution.

Other Ideas:

Science - ecological systems, elements, compounds, mixtures

Social Studies - causes of the American Revolution, causes of the Civil War, characteristics of various colonies, famous people of a given time period

Language Arts - major events in a plot

Collage
Literary Collage

NAME_____

Your task is to create a collage showing the literary elements of character, setting, plot, conflict and resolution from a short story or novel you have read.

Directions:

1. Take a sheet of construction paper and draw eight shapes: they can be rectangles, squares, circles or any combination.
2. Behind each shape, glue notebook paper or white drawing paper. (It's nice to use a colored sheet of paper for this.)
3. In one section of the collage, you will place the title and author of the story or novel.
4. Select one section to label "Character." In this section you will give the name of a character from the story and describe this character.
5. Select another section to label "Setting." Describe one setting from the story.
6. Select another section to label "Plot." (Use the largest section of the collage for this section because you will be placing a brief summary of the story's highlights here.)
7. Label another section "Conflict/Resolution." In this section you will describe the main conflict in the piece you read, and you will tell how the conflict was resolved.
8. The final two sections will be used for you to show illustrations about the story.
9. Decorate the collage frame. Make sure your name is on the back of the collage.

Rubric for Literary Collage:

_____ title and author are provided in one section (5 points)

_____ character is vividly described (10 points)

_____ setting is vividly described (10 points)

_____ plot summary includes highlights of the story (10 points)

_____ main conflict of the story is described (10 points)

_____ resolution to the main conflict is described (10 points)

_____ two illustrations are provided and labeled (10 points)

_____ correct grammar, spelling, punctuation, capitalization, complete sentences (15 points)

_____ collage frame is neatly decorated/ neat, attractive presentation (20 points)

_____ FINAL GRADE/100

Collage
Literary Collage

Teacher Page

This is a familiar and fun format for your students. Give the typical photo collage format a new twist by asking students to organize the five sections of the collage to represent literary elements.

Project Description: After reading a short story or novel, students will be instructed to create a collage representing the literary elements.

Materials:

___construction paper
___notebook paper

___white drawing paper
___markers, crayons, colored pencils

Suggestions:
• Allow students class time to prepare their rough drafts. Once they are complete, encourage students to proofread each other's papers. They can then transfer their final pieces onto the collage.
• The completed collage can be decorated using ideas from the story they read. For example, an animal story might be decorated with pictures of the animal or a story taking place in the mountains might be decorated with pictures of mountains.
• Stickers, bows, or puffy paints also make colorful decorations.

Other Ideas:
Collages can visually represent just about any science or social studies concept you are teaching.

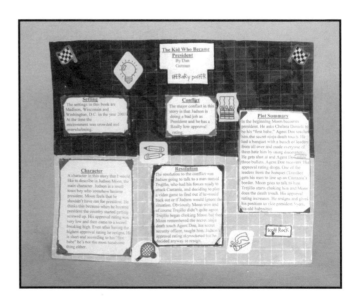

Diorama
3-D Diorama

NAME_____

Build one of your favorite settings from a story with everyday materials and then write a detailed description of it.

Directions:

1. Select the box you will use, and make the background. You could color, paint, or glue construction paper inside to look like the sky, ground, or some other aspect of the background.
2. You must have at least one item to make the setting 3-D. You could use twigs to make a tree, cotton for clouds, aluminum foil for water. Be creative and have fun!
3. Write a description of the scene you've created and glue it on to the top of the box. Remember to put the title and author of the story you read.
4. Make sure your name is visible somewhere on the box.

Rubric for 3-D Diorama:

_____ written description vividly describes setting from the story; title and author are noted; written description using correct grammar, punctuation, capitalization, spelling, complete sentences (25 points)

_____ scene created is 3-D; diorama is neat/attractive; your name is visible (25 points)

_____ FINAL GRADE/50 points

Diorama
3-D Diorama

Teacher Page

Allow your students to recreate their favorite scenes from a short story, novel, or nonfiction book by constructing a three-dimensional set using everyday materials from home.

Project Description: Students will construct a 3-D setting in a box and write a detailed description of that setting.

Materials:
___box (a shoebox works well)   ___construction paper
___crayons, markers, and/or paint   ___glue

Suggestions:
- Encourage students to sketch the scene on paper before designing the diorama.
- A shoebox works well for this project. Encourage students to be creative: empty toilet paper and paper towel rolls, small cans, or other items they bring in from home are all useful.

Other Ideas:

Science - local habitats

Social Studies - geographical place, historical events

Envelope
Theme Envelope

Your task is to pick one theme from a short story or novel you have read and find examples of that theme in another story, in a movie, TV, or even from real life.

Directions:

1. Select a theme and cite specific examples of events in the story that illustrate this theme.
2. On the outside flap of a large, letter-sized envelope, write the title and author of the story read.
3. On the address side of the envelope, write the theme from the story and provide an illustration of this theme that relates to the story.
4. Prepare two cards to place inside the envelope. On each card, describe an event that relates to the theme. These events can be personal experiences or examples from other literature selections, movies, or television shows.
5. On the reverse side of the card, illustrate this theme based on the written description. Place the cards in the envelope.
6. Write your name on the blank side of the envelope.

Rubric for Theme Envelope:

_____title and author are written on the outside flap of the envelope (5 points)

_____theme is written on the front of the envelope and relates to the story; illustration demonstrates theme (10 points)

_____card one describes an example of this theme; illustration demonstrates theme (10 points)

_____card two describes another example of this theme; illustration demonstrates theme (10 points)

_____correct use of grammar, spelling, punctuation, capitalization, complete sentences (10 points)

_____your name is on the blank side of the envelope (5 points)

_____FINAL GRADE/50

Envelope
Theme Envelope

Teacher Page

This project helps students grasp the abstract concept of theme by first applying it to their own lives and then looking for it in the literature they've read.

Project Description: Students will create an envelope containing cards that demonstrate the themes in a short story or novel. These cards will be illustrated and placed in the envelope.

Materials:
___one large letter-size envelope
___2 index cards

___markers, crayons, and/or colored pencils

Suggestions:
- After reading a short story or novel, elicit a class discussion on the various themes that run throughout the story. List these themes on the board or on a chart. Then, briefly discuss how these themes can be found in real life. After students choose a theme to work on, you will ask them to develop two examples of how this theme relates to life in general. Here they can cite personal examples or use examples from other literature selections, movies, or television shows that illustrate the theme. The number of cards can vary depending on your students' needs and the topic chosen.
- An alternate way to present the cards is to put a hole in the top and bottom of each card (except the bottom of the last card), string them together with yarn, and hang them as a mobile. For this presentation method, students should mark one card with the title and author on one side and their names on the other.

Other Ideas:
Language Arts - After reading a short story or novel, each student will develop a set of five cards with one side describing information pertinent to the character and the other side showing an illustration. The cards could contain a character's physical attributes, personality, behavior, thoughts and feelings, what others think of the character, a conflict the character was involved in, and how this conflict was resolved.

Essay
The Many Faces of Literature

NAME_____

Pick a character and list his/her characteristics on chart paper. Then, work with classmates to find characters that are similar to yours and explain how they are similar in a short essay.

Directions:

1. Select a favorite character from a book you've read.
2. Develop a chart showing the character's physical attributes, personality, behavior, thoughts and feelings, and what others think of the character.
3. Find another person in class who has a character with similar personalities, behaviors, thoughts and feelings. Compare the characteristics of both characters.
4. After learning about each other's characters, you will work together to write one essay explaining why your characters could be friends (or how they are similar). Include specific incidents from both your stories to describe how the characters are similar.
5. Once you complete your essay, draw a picture of the way you see your characters using the physical attributes shown on your chart.
6. Be sure to place the characters' names above or below each character and the title and author of the book on your essay.
7. Paste your essay near your characters on a large sheet of paper.
8. Turn in your chart with your essay and illustration.

Rubric for The Many Faces of Literature:

_____ essay describes characters' similarities in personality, behavior, and thoughts and feelings and what others think of the character by providing specific examples from the story (15 points)

_____ essay is written using correct grammar, spelling, punctuation, capitalization, complete sentences; evidence of varied sentence structure and use of transitions (15 points)

_____ illustrations show characters' physical attributes from chart (10 points)

_____ your names are written on the essay; characters' names, title and author of the story are clearly presented (10 points)

_____ FINAL GRADE/50

Essay
The Many Faces of Literature

Teacher Page

In this project, your students will learn to make comparisons across several pieces of literature, an important step towards literary critique.

Project Description: Students will develop a characterization chart for one character and then find another students' characterization chart with similar characteristics listed. Those students will then write an essay on what makes their characters similar.

Materials:
___chart paper
___notebook paper

___markers, crayons, or colored
pencils

Suggestions:
Generate a class discussion about people's characteristics in real life. Discuss the ways in which characters in books or on television are fictional people, then have students think of the ways specific characters from books and television shows resemble the characters in the stories and novels they have read. After students have found similar characters, ask them to form groups of three or four based on their characters' similarities. Students should discuss the similarities and each write an essay comparing similarities and differences. Once the essays are completed, provide students with a large sheet of paper. (This can be white bulletin board paper or pieces of construction paper which students can tape together.) It's also fun to use a ten-foot-long roll of paper and have a number of students do their illustrations, pasting their essays between their characters.

Other Ideas:
Science - comparing attributes of plants or animals

Social Studies - many faces of history

Flip Book
Literary Elements Flip Book

NAME_____

Using just a few sheets of construction paper, in this project you will label and illustrate the five literary elements of the piece you read.

Directions:

1. Line up sheets of construction paper and stagger them at 1" intervals in a vertical row.
2. Fold each sheet away from you, making sure each fold leaves 1" of paper above it.
3. Open the book to the center fold and staple. You now have a flip book.
4. Turn the flip book toward you. The top fold should include the title and author of the piece you read.
5. On the second flap, write the word "Character." Above it, describe a character from the story.
6. On the third flap, write the word "Setting." On this flap describe a setting from the story.
7. The fourth flap will have the word "Conflict/Resolution." Tell about a conflict in the story and how it was resolved.
8. The fifth flap will be labeled "Plot." Describe the important events that occur in the piece
9. The final flap will be titled "Critique." Give your opinion of the story, giving reasons why you liked or disliked the story, using specific details.
10. Write your name on the back of the flip book.

Rubric for Flip Book:

_____ title and author on first flap; your name on the back of the flip book (5 points)

_____ character description includes character's physical attributes, personality, behavior, thoughts and feelings, and what others think of the character; entry labeled "Character" (15 points)

_____ setting described using vivid vocabulary; entry labeled "Setting" (15 points)

_____ conflict/resolution described; entry labeled "Conflict/Resolution" (15 points)

_____ plot included important events occurring in the story; entry labeled "Plot" (15 points)

_____ critique uses specific details telling why you liked or disliked story; entry labeled "Critique" (15 points)

_____ correct spelling, usage, punctuation, capitalization, complete sentences; neatly presented (20 points)

_____ FINAL GRADE/100

Flip Book
Literary Elements Flip Book

Teacher Page

These books are a fun variation of the standard, bound book report. The segments allow for an organized division of information.

Project Description: After completing a story, novel, or nonfiction book, students will create a flip book. Each section of the flip book will detail one literary element or nonfiction feature under study. The last section will include a critique of the piece read. Adapt the rubric as needed based on the type of flip book.

Materials:
___3 sheets of construction paper (5" W X 8¹/²" H)
___crayons, markers, and/or colored pencils
___stapler

Suggestions:
- As students do this project, they might want to modify the size of their flip books.
- Depending on the topic chosen, students may need time to research the topic in the library before preparing their flip books.
- instead of stapling along the center fold, they can use a big needle with dental floss to secure the pages at the fold.

Other Ideas:

Language Arts - Each section of their flip book could describe an event from the plot of a story read. Students can make flip books for vocabulary words and definitions.

Science - Use the flip book to help students describe and illustrate the layers of the atmosphere; an animal, its habitat, habits, prey or role in the food chain; or parts of a plant.

Social Studies - Students can create a travelogue for a state or a country, describing the geography, weather, imports and exports, holidays, places to visit, population, holidays, education, and government.

Footprints
Follow the Footprints

NAME_____

Use your feet! Here you'll make a set of footprints out of construction paper and on them list and describe a sequence of events in the order they occurred.

Directions:

1. First, sequentially list the major events that take place in the short story, novel, or informational text, developing each one by describing the details of the event.
2. Cut seven footprints out of construction paper.
3. The first footprint will show the title and author of the story.
4. The rest of the footprints will have one event featured on each of them and should be numbered in the order that the events occurred in the story.
5. Decorate each footprint with illustrations showing the event described.
6. Display your footprints in the order the events occurred on a poster board.
7. Write your name on the back of the poster board.

Rubric for Follow the Footprints:

_____first footprint shows title and author (5 points)

_____footprint one completely describes an event taking place at the beginning of the piece (10 points)

_____footprint two completely describes an event following footprint one (10 points)

_____footprint three completely describes an event following footprint two (10 points)

_____footprint four completely describes an event following footprint three (10 points)

_____footprint five completely describes an event following footprint four (10 points)

_____footprint six completely describes an event following footprint five (10 points)

_____footprints are illustrated to show events described (10 points)

_____correct use of grammar, spelling, punctuation, capitalization, complete sentences (15 points)

_____footprints are numbered in the order the events occurred in the text (5 points)

_____your name is on the back of each footprint (5 points)

_____FINAL GRADE/100

Footprints
Follow the Footprints

Teacher Page

Let their feet do the teaching! This versatile project allows you to keep any curriculum unit moving forward fast!

Project Description: Students will describe the major events taking place in the piece they read and display them on a series of footprints.

Materials:
___7 footprint cutouts on construction paper
___poster board

___markers, crayons, or colored pencils
___glue

Suggestions:
• Students can trace their own footprint, cut it out and use it as a pattern or you can have patterns that the students trace.
• This project also works well as a group project. Each member is responsible for one or more footprints.
• You can alter the number of footprints (and the points in the rubric) to fit your students' needs.

Other Ideas:

Language Arts - Students can describe the events leading up to a conflict in a story and the events leading to its resolution. Footprints can be used to describe comma rules or to write a conversation to reinforce the use of quotation marks.

Science - Students can show the sequence of events in the formation of a volcano, in the process of erosion, the stages of the water cycle, or the formation of a fossil.

Social Studies - To describe the sequence of events leading up to the colonists rebelling against England or the reasons why the colonists left England for life in a new land. Students can also show the events leading up to the American Revolution.

Internet
Put It on the Web

NAME_____

In this project, you will have the opportunity to post your own literary review on the Internet.

Directions:

1. Go to www.amazon.com.
2. In the "Search" box, select "Books" then click "Go."
3. Type in the title and author of the book and click "Search Now."
4. When you find your title, click on it.
5. Scroll down to "All Customer Reviews." At this point, you may want to read several reviews. When you're ready to write, click on "Write an online review," or, if you're under 13, click on "Use our kid's review form."
6. Scroll down to the textbox, rate the book using a five-star scale, give your review a title, and type a review of no more than 1000 words.
7. Your review must include a mention of specific events in the plot, the setting, a conflict and its resolution
8. You can then preview what you've written and then either edit or save.
9. Print the review and turn it in. Make sure your name is on it.

Rubric for Put It on the Web:

_____your name is on the review (5 points)

_____review describes specific events of the plot (10 points)

_____review makes reader aware of the setting (10 points)

_____review clearly states a conflict and its resolution (10 points)

_____correct use of grammar, spelling, punctuation, capitalization, complete sentences (15 points)

_____FINAL GRADE/50

Internet
Put It on the Web

Teacher Page

Have your students hone their computer skills while learning how to write a literary review—two skills that will be indispensable throughout their school careers.

Project Description: After reading a novel, students will publish a review of that novel on the website, www.amazon.com.

Materials:
___computer with Internet access   ___printer

Suggestions:
- Students under 13 can use the kid's forum, which allows them to post a review without being asked for a name or an email address.
- Students 13 and over must type in an e-mail address and sign in. The student will register by creating a password then will click "Continue." The next screen will tell the student that he has successfully signed in and will instruct him to click "Continue" to write a review.
- It is helpful if students read several reviews already posted on amazon.com. (Your students will notice that their reviews read better than most because they're being graded.)

Letter
Letter to a Friend

NAME_____

In this project you will write a letter to a friend describing a character using examples from the book or short story you read.

Directions:

1. Pick someone in class to whom you would like to write a letter.
2. From your chosen book, pick a character that you will write a letter about. Imagine this character is a new friend.
3. Begin this letter by telling your classmate that you have a new friend. You will give the character's name and the title and author of the book where you met this character.
4. Then describe the character to the person to whom you are writing. You will describe the character's physical attributes, personality (how he or she thinks and feels), how the character behaves, and what others think of the character.
5. You will want to cite specific incidents from the book to describe the character's personality, behavior, thoughts, and feelings.
6. Your letter must use the correct format for a friendly letter.

Rubric for Letter to a Friend:

_____ correct friendly letter format is used, which includes a heading, greeting, body, and closing (10 points)

_____ body of letter describes the character's physical attributes; examples from the story help to describe character's personality, behavior, thoughts and feelings, and what others think of the character (20 points)

_____ correct use of grammar, punctuation, spelling, complete sentences (15 points)

_____ letter is written legibly; neat in appearance (5 points)

_____ FINAL GRADE/50

Letter
Letter to a Friend

Teacher Page

This project incorporates several lessons in one: letter writing, audience awareness (a component of voice), and characterization

Project Description: After reading a short story or novel, students select a character that they admire. Then each student will write a letter to a friend, describing this character.

Materials:
___paper   ___pen or pencil

Suggestions:
To introduce this assignment, a brief lesson on the conventions of a friendly letter should be taught (heading, greeting, body, signed closing). If this project is used for science or social studies, students may need a class period or two in the school media center to research the person they admire.

Other Ideas:
<u>Language Arts</u> - Students can write a letter to a friend describing a poet or an author. This project can also be used with the Character Cutout (Paper Doll) project (see p. 51).

<u>Science</u> - Students can write letters describing famous scientists or inventors.

<u>Social Studies</u> - Students can write letters describing explorers, great leaders, heroes, or presidents.

Milk Carton
Milk Carton Mobile

NAME_____

Your task is to create a milk carton display providing information on a given topic of nonfiction study. Each side of the carton will display a written description of a major component of your studies, along with an illustration.

Directions:

1. Bring a clean, four-sided milk carton from home. Paint it at home if possible.
2. Decorate your carton using wrapping paper, wallpaper, or contact paper.
3. Write the title of your project on a strip of construction paper and glue it to the top of the carton. Write your name on the bottom of the carton.
4. Plan out the space on each side of the carton so you will have room for a label, a description, and an illustration.
5. Create labels for each side of the carton and glue them on.
6. Write a description of each of the four topics and glue these on.
7. Create illustrations for each description and glue them on.
8. Punch a hole in the pouring spout of the carton and thread string or yarn through it. Cartons can now be hung for display.

Rubric for Nonfiction Milk Carton Mobile:

_____carton is painted or covered attractively (5 points)

_____project title is on the top of the carton; your name is on the bottom (5 points)

_____each section of the carton contains a title and a well-written description or thorough research; panel is illustrated

_____panel 1 (15 points)

_____panel 2 (15 points)

_____panel 3 (15 points)

_____panel 4 (15 points)

_____correct use of grammar, spelling, punctuation, capitalization, complete sentences (20 points)

_____neat/attractive presentation (10 points)

_____FINAL GRADE/100

Milk Carton
Milk Carton Mobile

Teacher Page

These milk carton mobiles are fun and easy to make and can be used in many ways. Encourage your students to be creative when they are choosing their topics.

Project Description: Students will respond to a nonfiction unit of study by preparing milk cartons that depict four major components of the unit.

Materials:
___one milk carton per student (they can bring them in from home)
___paint, contact paper, wallpaper, or wrapping paper
___markers, crayons, colored pencils
___construction paper
___glue
___hole puncher
___string or yarn

Suggestions:
Paper milk cartons are the easiest to use for this project. If students are able, have them paint their cartons at home, or cover their cartons with wallpaper, wrapping paper, or contact paper.

Other Ideas:
Language Arts - Students can describe major events of a fictional plot or illustrate four literary elements.

Science - Students can describe various aspects of kingdoms, planets, biomes, or layers of the earth.

Social Studies - students can display information on early civilization, states, countries, continents, colonies, or human rights issues

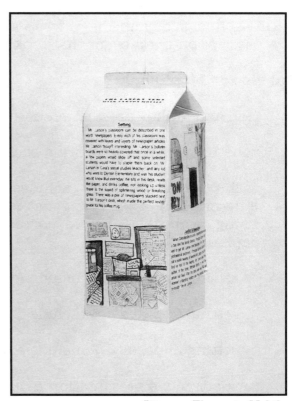

Literary Elements Mobile

Mini-Book
Dear Diary Mini-Book

NAME_____

Your task is to create a mini-book diary discussing the settings in the story you have just read and the events that took place at these settings. You will write your diaries in the first person as if you were experiencing the setting by being there.

Directions:

1. Holding your construction paper with the 18" side at the top, fold the paper in half from left to right.
2. Make your second fold from top to bottom.
3. Open your paper back up. You should have eight equal segments.
4. Now fold your paper in half from left to right again.
5. Make a cut on the horizontal center crease, starting from the left side of your folded paper. Cut only to the center of the paper.
6. Open up your paper again. Now fold it from the 18" top side to the bottom. The cut you made should now be on the top fold.
7. Hold your paper with one hand on each end of the paper and push inward. The pieces will come together to make four equal segments. You now have a mini book with four pages.
8. On the front of your mini diary, write the title and author of the book you have just read. Write your name on the back of the diary.
9. On each page of your diary, write a vivid description of a setting in the story and a description of an event that took place there on each page of your diary.

Rubric for Mini-Book:

_____title and author are written on the front (page 1) of the mini diary (5 points)

_____your name is written on the back (page 8) of the diary (5 points)

_____each page of your diary includes a vivid description of a place in the story and a description of the event that took place at this setting; entries are written using complete sentences, correct grammar, spelling, punctuation, and capitalization.

_____setting 1: pages 2-3 include a description and illustration (10 points)

_____setting 2: pages 4-5 include a description and illustration (10 points)

_____setting 3: pages 6-7 include a description and illustration (10 points)

_____neat/attractive presentation (10 points)

_____FINAL GRADE/50

Mini-Book
Dear Diary Mini-Book

Teacher Page

Diaries are a great way for students to express their thoughts about the short story or novel they have just read.

Project Description: After reading a short story or novel with the class, lead a class discussion about the various settings. Students will be creating a diary and writing descriptions of the settings from the story in the first person as if they had actually visited them.

Materials:
___one sheet of 12" x 18" construction paper for each student

___scissors
___crayons, markers, colored pencils

Suggestions:
- Brainstorm with your students to develop a list of all the settings in book or story. You might want to discuss what happened at each setting to refresh your students' memories and give them some vivid details to work with.
- Students could write in their diaries during class or as a homework assignment.

Other Ideas:

Language Arts - Students can dedicate one page to each literary element or use the whole book to write about one specific element. Students can make a photo essay of several chapters and then draw pictures to show highlights of the plot for each section read.
- Each student takes on the role of a character and writes from that point of view.

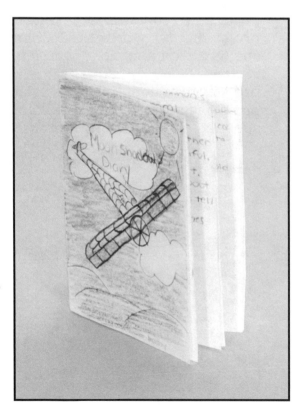

Science - Students can display information on kingdoms, body systems, the solar system, plants, or any unit of study.

Social Studies - Students can describe great leaders of an era, world religions, ancient civilizations, or they could present a timeline with a date and description on each page.

Mini-Museum
Multi-Genre Project

NAME_____

Your task is to complete a series of three projects. Be sure to give each project a title and place your name on each component of your project. Each component should be colorful and attractive.

Select any three projects in the book:

1. Mobile or collage of events related to your topic.
2. Booklet of famous people associated with your topic (you can use a flip book or accordion book).
3. Song or poem about your topic.
4. Newspaper article related to your topic.
5. Business letter or letter to the editor of the newspaper that deals with your topic.

Rubric for Multi-Genre Project:

_____each project is titled and includes your name (10 points)

_____project one contains facts related to your topic; evidence of concise research; project is neatly presented, colorful and attractive; correct use of grammar, spelling, capitalization, complete sentences (30 points)

_____project two contains facts related to your topic; evidence of concise research; project is neatly presented, colorful and attractive; correct use of grammar, spelling, capitalization, complete sentences (30 points)

_____project three contains facts related to your topic; evidence of concise research; project is neatly presented, colorful and attractive; correct use of grammar, spelling, capitalization, complete sentences (30 points)

_____FINAL GRADE/100

Mini-Museum
Multi-Genre Project

Teacher Page

For an interdisciplinary unit or to integrate a nonfiction topic with a fictional story, provide students with the student page which includes a variety of suggested projects.

Project Description: At your discretion, either assign specific projects to meet your individual objectives or allow students to select three projects in order to supply information of their given topics.

Materials:
(vary by projects selected)

Suggestions:
Projects can be set up to form a mini-museum. Students from other classes can be invited to view the projects. Projects can also be displayed for a parent night. If your media center has space, display the projects there.

Other Ideas:
This versatile projects allows you freedom to combine books, topics, or genres, using several media.

Mini-Poster
Theme Mini-Poster

NAME_____

Your task is to create a mini-poster illustrating a theme from a short story or novel you read that also occurs in other pieces of literature, movies, television shows, or real life situations.

Directions:

1. Pick one theme from the piece you read and write the theme at the top of a mini poster.
2. Divide the poster into four sections. Label the first section with the title and author of the story you read. Write a description of how this theme relates to the story; illustrate your description.
3. Label the other three sections with the title of other stories, movies, television shows, or real-life situations that relate to this theme. In each section, describe how this theme relates to the situation labeled in that section. Illustrate each section.
4. Remember to put your name on the back of your poster.

Rubric for Theme Mini Poster:

_____theme is written on the top of the mini poster (5 points)

_____first section includes title and author of the piece read, a description of how the theme relates to this piece, and an illustration (15 points)

_____second section includes name of movie, literature selection, television show, or real-life situation that relates to this theme, a description of how the theme relates to this event, and an illustration (15 points)

_____third section includes name of movie, literature selection, television show, or real-life situation that relates to this theme, a description of how the theme relates to this event, and an illustration (15 points)

_____fourth section includes name of movie, literature selection, television show, or real-life situation that relates to this theme, a description of how the theme relates to this event, and an illustration (15 points)

_____correct use of grammar, spelling, punctuation, capitalization, complete sentences (20 points)

_____neat/attractive presentation (10 points)

_____your name is on the back of the poster (5 points)

_____FINAL GRADE/100

Mini-Poster
Theme Mini-Poster

Teacher Page

This space-saving project helps your students make connections among various media while learning the concept of theme. You can also use the mini-poster to teach sequencing of events or division of a topic into its components.

Project Description: Students will create a mini-poster illustrating the theme(s) that are evident in a short story or novel read.

Materials:
___construction paper or tag board

___markers, crayons, and/or colored pencils

Suggestions:
Explain to students how themes are universal and occur in literature, television shows, movies, and even throughout our lives. After a class discussion of the theme(s) in a short story or novel read, list these themes on the board or a chart. Lead a discussion about where these themes appear in other pieces of literature, television shows, movies, and real life situations.

Other Ideas:
Language Arts - Plot: Major events in a short story or novel can be described and illustrated in four parts.

Science - Plants: Divide mini-poster into segments to describe and illustrate parts of a plant.

Social Studies - A sequence of historical events can be described and illustrated in four parts.

Mobile
Plot Mobile

NAME_____

Your task is to create a mobile on which you will hang cards that describe major events in the plot of a story you have just read.

Directions:

1. Trace the triangle shape of the inside of the hanger onto construction paper.
2. Cut out the triangle and punch a hole in each of the three corners. Thread ribbon or yarn through each hole and tie the triangle of construction paper to the inside area of your hanger.
3. On one side of the triangle you will write the title and author of the story you read. On the other side you will write your name.
4. Using construction paper, make cards to hang from your hanger. Write a description of one of the major events on one side of a card. On the other side you will provide an illustration of this event. Repeat for each of the four major events. Be sure to number your cards in the order the events occurred in the story.
5. Punch a hole in the top center of each card and use ribbon or yarn to fasten the card to your hanger. Once a card is tied to the hanger, secure it with a piece of tape so it doesn't slide around.

Rubric for Plot Mobile:

_____title and author are written in the center of the hanger (5 points)

_____your name is on the other side of the triangle (5 points)

_____card one contains a complete description of event one; illustration on reverse side (15 points)

_____card two contains a well-developed description of an event occurring after event one; illustration on reverse side (15 points)

_____card three contains a well-developed description of an event occurring after event two; illustration on reverse side (15 points)

_____card four contains a well-developed description of an event occurring after event three; illustration on reverse side (15 points)

_____correct use of grammar, spelling, punctuation, capitalization, complete sentences (20 points)

_____neat/attractive appearance (10 points)

_____FINAL GRADE/100

Mobile
Plot Mobile

Teacher Page

Mobiles are a creative way to decorate your classroom and to display information about your unit or current topic of study.

Project Description: Students will describe and illustrate four major events taking place in a short story or novel. They will display the information on cards attached to a hanger to create a mobile.

Materials:
___ one wire clothes hanger per student
(have students bring from home)
___ construction paper
___ markers, crayons, colored pencils
___ scissors
___ hole-puncher
___ yarn or ribbon
___ cellophane tape

Suggestions:
• Creative students might want to cut their construction paper cards into various shapes that enhance their descriptions.
• Have students brainstorm and then make a list of the four major events of the story, develop these ideas and be ready to write descriptions of them before they begin their projects.

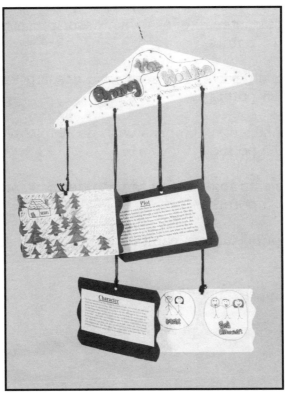
Literary Elements Mobile

Monument
Worthy of Mt. Rushmore

NAME_____

In this project, you will recreate Mt. Rushmore using the heads of important characters from a story or novel you have just read. You will select four characters from the story, draw or glue their faces on your mountain, and write a brief description of each figure.

Directions:
1. Paste your likeness of Mt. Rushmore onto a piece of paper.
2. On the top of your paper place the title and author of the short story or novel you read.
3. Determine the four characters from the story who are worthy of being placed on your mountain.
4. You will draw (or cut out and glue) pictures of each character's head to fit its assigned space on the mountain.
5. Underneath each head you will write a brief description explaining the character's accomplishment and why it made him worthy of this position.
6. Write your name on the reverse side of your paper.

Rubric for Worthy of Mt. Rushmore:

_____title and author of story is at the top of paper (5 points)

_____first head shows character likeness with description of character's accomplishment (15 points)

_____second head shows character likeness with description of character's accomplishment (15 points)

_____third head shows character likeness with description of character's accomplishment (15 points)

_____fourth head shows character likeness with description of character's accomplishment (15 points)

_____correct grammar, punctuation, capitalization, spelling, complete sentences (20 points)

_____project is neat in appearance (15 points)

_____your name is on the reverse side (5 points)

_____FINAL GRADE/100

Monument
Worthy of Mt. Rushmore

Teacher Page

Mt. Rushmore is a fascinating piece of U.S. history. Take a little time to get your students into the spirit of the project by explaining the significance of the mountain and the famous men carved into it.

Project Description: Tell students that they will be constructing a reproduction of Mt. Rushmore, replacing the famous heads carved on the mountain with the heads of important characters from a short story or novel they have read.

Materials:

___paper
___copy or outline of Mt. Rushmore
   (students can trace or draw a
   likeness)

___markers, crayons, colored pencils
___scissors
___glue

Suggestions:

Before beginning this lesson, you can read students an article from an encyclopedia or history book about Mt. Rushmore and the people carved on the mountain.

Other Ideas:

<u>Language Arts</u> - Students can use people involved in a classroom thematic unit study, poets from a poetry unit, or characters from a story.

<u>Science</u> - Students can use famous scientists, inventors, or people who made an impact in any area of science.

<u>Social Studies</u> - Students can use presidents, explorers, heroes, great people from a particular state or country, famous faces of World War I and World War II, or great leaders in U.S. history.

Heroic women in American history

Mural
Setting Mural

NAME_____

Your task is to create a piece of a mural depicting the setting in which an important part of the story or novel you read took place. You will work in a small group on a specific section of the story. It is your job to reread the section and determine the setting before you start.

Directions:

1. Across the top of a large piece of white bulletin board paper you will write the pages or chapters to which your group has been assigned.
2. As a group, decide on the setting of your section and agree on the images each person will illustrate in order to portray your section.
3. Illustrate your section. Get creative and use multiple media, such as markers, crayons, colored pencils, or paint.
4. On the bottom of your mural, you will write a brief description of what you are showing.
5. Your group will then paste each illustrated section on a larger sheet of bulletin board paper in the order in which it occurs in the story.
6. In the corner of the mural piece, each group member will write his or her name.

Rubric for Setting Mural:

_____mural is titled with chapters/pages illustrated (5 points)

_____mural colorfully depicts setting in assigned section (20 points)

_____description of setting is written at bottom of page; written description included correct grammar, punctuation, capitalization, spelling, complete sentences (10 points)

_____students worked together with each student sharing in responsibilities (10 points)

_____students' names are written on a bottom corner of their mural piece (5 points)

_____FINAL GRADE/50

Mural
Setting Mural

Teacher Page

Murals are a time-honored way to illustrate stories. In this project, your students use the mural to gain a visual sense of the setting of a story they have read.

Project Description:

Most short stories and novels have several settings. Tell your students that they will be recreating all the settings of the shared class story or book as a single mural.

Materials:
___ large sheets of white bulletin board paper
___ crayons, markers, colored pencils, paint (if you are brave)
___ glue

Suggestions:

• This project works well when a class is reading the same story or book. Each group is responsible for illustrating the setting in a section of a story, or in one or more chapters of a novel.

• First, divide the book or story into appropriate sections, and divide the class into that number of groups. Each student receives a copy of the rubric. Each group receives the final grade. The group is graded on how well they work together and to what extent each individual contributed to complete the mural section.

• The size and type of paper you use depends on the number of settings in the novel or story. Usually, a large piece of bulletin board paper works well if there are five or fewer settings. After the groups finish their sections, the groups paste on their sections in the order the settings appeared in the work during class discussions.

Other Ideas:

<u>Science</u> - Students can make a mural that illustrates the life cycle of a plant or animal.

<u>Social Studies</u> - Students can make a timeline mural of important historical dates.

Newspaper
Literary Newspaper

NAME_____

Your task is to write a series of articles, each one relating to a specific literary element. You can write informational articles, editorials, advertisements, a question/answer column, want ads, or any other piece that might be published in a newspaper. You will compile the pieces together to create a fun and informative newspaper.

Directions:

1. Each member of your group will be responsible for one or more articles. Write separate pieces describing the characters, the setting, the conflict, and possibly the theme of the story.
2. Draft your article. Peer-edit each other's papers to make sure the group agrees on the final pieces.
3. Take a large sheet of the bulletin board paper or tag board and fold it in half.
4. Decide on a name for your newspaper and write the name on the front cover of the folded board.
5. Paste the main articles on the front cover of the folded board and paste smaller articles inside.
6. Use markers, crayons, and colored pencils to decorate/illustrate your newspaper.

Rubric for Literary Newspaper:

_____ newspaper has a title and date of publication (5 points)

_____ your article addresses topic of study with a well-written piece that provides and adequate amount of information (15 points)

_____ article contains correct grammar, complete sentences, proper punctuation, capitalization, and correct spelling (15 points)

_____ article has a title and author (your name) (5 points)

_____ article is written neatly and legibly; illustrated (5 points)

_____ worked as a group to produce a neat/attractive product (5 points)

_____ FINAL GRADE/50

Newspaper
Literary Newspaper

Teacher Page

Creating a literary newspaper is a visual and concrete group project that allows students to explore the various elements of literature.

Project Description: Each group writes and assembles a literary newspaper that covers the five literary elements of a story or novel they have read.

Materials:
___large sheets of bulletin board or tag board

___markers, colored pencils, or crayons
___glue or cellophane tape

Suggestions:
• Divide students into groups with no more than seven students.
• Students should be encouraged to include other types of writing that appear in newspapers besides news articles, such as want ads, comics, advertisements, features, and advice and opinion columns. To introduce this project, it might be useful to review the different types of articles that appear in a newspaper or bring a newspaper in for students to see.
• The members of each group write their part of the newspaper and mount it on a large piece of bulletin board paper that is folded in half.
• Each student should be graded independently on his work.

Other Ideas:
Language Arts - Each article can correspond to a specific literary element.

Science - Students could create a newspaper on machines, the human body system, atoms and molecules, or ecosystems.

Social Studies - Students can write articles on ancient civilizations, any particular period in history, countries, or states.

Paper Bag
Plot Paper Bag

NAME_____

Your task is to create a paper bag containing cutouts describing the major events that took place in a short story or novel you read. You can draw shapes of people, buildings, animals, or objects that appear in the story.

Directions:

1. Make a list of six important events that took place in the story.
2. Take your idea and turn it into a shape. You can draw shapes of people, buildings, animals or things in the story.
3. Cut out the shapes and write a description of the event on the back of the shape.
4. Put the shapes in the order that they happened in the story and number them on the back.
5. Put all the shapes in the paper bag and now decorate the front of the paper bag with a design about the book. Make sure to write the title and author of the story.
6. Don't forget to write your name on the bottom of the bag.

Rubric for Paper Bag:

_____ title and author on the front of a paper bag; your name is on the bottom (5 points)

_____ cutout one completely describes an event taking place at the beginning of the story (10 points)

_____ cutout two completely describes an event taking place after cut out one (10 points)

_____ cutout three completely describes an event taking place after cut out two (10 points)

_____ cutout four completely describes an event taking place after cut out three (10 points)

_____ cutout five completely describes an event taking place after cut out four (10 points)

_____ cutout six completely describes an event taking place after cut out five (10 points)

_____ cutouts are numbered in the order the events occurred in the story. (5 points)

_____ use of correct grammar, punctuation, capitalization, spelling, complete sentences. (20 points)

_____ outside of bag provides a new book jacket (10 points)

_____ FINAL GRADE/10

Paper Bag
Plot Paper Bag

Teacher Page

It's in the bag! Students fill simple paper bags with creative cutouts that relate to or describe the plot of a short story or novel. They learn to translate their knowledge and understanding of the story into a fun project. Your students are sure to remember these stories.

Project Description: After completing a short story or novel, students will describe the major events in the plot by filling a paper bag with fun cutout shapes.

Materials:
___lunch-size paper bags
___construction paper
___markers, crayons, colored pencils
___scissors

Suggestions:
• This project lends itself especially well to nonfiction topics. The cutouts can relate to any phase of the study at hand.
• The front of the bag can be decorated to represent a new book cover.
• The contents of the bag can be simple 3" x 5" cards, or the students can create cutouts that represent characters or concepts found in the book.

Other Ideas:
Science - Students can write on topics related to weather, creating shapes for cloud types, lightning bolts, raindrops, snow, etc.

Social Studies - Students can write about topics ranging from foreign cultures, military history, the Depression, or ancient civilizations.

Theme Paper Bag

Paper Doll
Character Cutout

NAME_____

Your task is to create a cutout character representing one of the characters in a short story or novel you have read. You will need to look through magazines and cut out pictures that look like the character.

Directions:

1. Choose a character from the story that your teacher assigns.
2. Look through magazines to find a face that you imagine your character would have and cut the picture out.
3. Next look for a body that you imagine the character might have and also cut this picture out.
4. Paste the picture of your character's face on the body
5. You will then want to dress your character appropriately for the story. If the character used any props, such as sports equipment, tools, furniture, or if he or she had a pet or other special item, you might want to cut this out and place it also on the page.
6. Once you have made your character, write a description on the back. You will want to describe the character's physical attributes as well as the character's personality, behavior, thoughts and feelings, and what others think of the character.

Rubric for Character Cutout:

_____ character cutout matches the written description which describes character's physical attributes, behavior, thoughts, and feelings, and what others think of this character. (25 points)

_____ paragraph is written using correct spelling, punctuation, capitalization, usage, complete sentences (25 points)

_____ ideas are connected using transitions; written with a mature command of the language (25 points)

_____ character cutout and description are neatly presented (25 points)

_____ your name is visible on the project

_____ FINAL GRADE/100

Paper Doll
Character Cutout

Teacher Page

Characters come to life! In this project students create real images of their favorite characters from the story they read. Students interpret the character's personality to create fun and original images.

Project Description: After reading a short story or novel, students will select a character to describe and illustrate.

Materials:
___magazines
___construction paper
___pen or pencil
___glue
___scissors

Suggestions:
Encourage your students to use vivid verbs and specific adjectives.

Other Ideas:
<u>Social Studies</u> - Students can choose to depict a person they admire most. It can be a political leader, athlete, scientist, or a person in their life. They can create their own descriptions and list the qualities they admire.

Paper Plate

NAME_____

Your task is to create a plate on which you describe a topic of study. You will divide the plate into four parts in order to describe the different aspects.

Directions:

1. Before you begin writing on your plate, you will want to decide on four aspects of the topic that you want to describe.
2. You will then describe each idea and provide a title,
3. Once you are done with your rough draft and have proofread and edited it, you are ready to transfer your information onto your paper plate.
4. Divide the plate into four sections and transfer your title and descriptions onto each section.
5. Write the title of your project along the rim of the plate.
6. Provide illustrations where space allows and write your name on the back.

Rubric for Paper Plate:

_____ project's title is on the plate's rim (5 points)

_____ section one is labeled and contains a well written description of your topic (15 points)

_____ section two is labeled and contains a well written description of your topic (15 points)

_____ section three is labeled and contains a well written description of your topic (15 points)

_____ section four is labeled and contains a well written description of your topic (15 points)

_____ correct use of grammar, spelling, punctuation, capitalization, complete sentences (20 points)

_____ neat/attractive presentation; illustrations provided where space is available (10 points)

_____ your name is on the back of the plate (5 points)

_____ FINAL GRADE/100

Paper Plate

Paper plates are no longer just for dinner! Turn ordinary paper plates into a creative outlet for understanding topics. Students artistically describe aspects of study on four sections of a simple paper plate.

Project Description: Students will describe various aspects of a current unit of study and then place the information on a paper plate to be displayed.

Materials:
___paper plates   ___crayons
___markers   ___colored pencils

Suggestions:
* Use this project to help students understand main ideas, a skill that many find difficult.
* can also be used for character development by dividing into four descriptive parts: physical attributes, behavior, thoughts and feelings, and what others think of the character.

Other Ideas:

Language Arts - Students can describe two conflicts and their resolutions. Students can discuss the themes in a story. Students can provide examples and describe figurative language in stories or poems.

Science - Students can describe compounds, elements, research who, what, when and where for scientists or inventors; describe properties of matter.

Social Studies - Students can describe aspects of culture, world religions, ancient civilizations, and causes of a war.

Pizza
Plot Pizza

NAME_____

Your task is to create a pizza that retells the plot of a short story or novel that you have read. You will need to think of six important events that occur in the story, which will be mounted onto slices of your pizza.

Directions:
1. After reading, list six important events that happened in the story in the order in which they occurred.
2. Write a rough draft of the list of events and proofread.
3. Construct your pizza, cutting a piece of tag board, construction paper, or poster board into a circle.
4. Divide the circle into six equal pieces. Number the slices from one to six.
5. Write one event on each slice in the order they occurred in the story.
6. Decorate each slice with hand-drawn illustrations, computer graphics, or images cut out from magazines. Shred paper to represent onions, green pepper, pepperoni, and other pizza toppings.
7. If your teacher gives you a box, place the pizza in it, and write your name and the book title and author name on the bottom of the box. If you do not have a box, write your name and the book title and author name on the back of the pizza.

Rubric for Plot Pizza:
_____title, author, and your name are on project (5 points)

_____slice one describes an event at the beginning of the story; illustrated (10 points)

_____slice two describes an event coming after event one; illustrated (10 points)

_____slice three describes an event coming after event two; illustrated (10 points)

_____slice four describes an event coming after event three; illustrated (10 points)

_____slice five describes an event coming after event four; illustrated (10 points)

_____slice six describes an event coming after event five; illustrated (10 points)

_____correct use of grammar, spelling, punctuation, complete sentences (20 points)

_____toppings are added for effect (5 points)

_____neat/attractive appearance (10 points)

_____FINAL GRADE/100

Pizza
Plot Pizza

Teacher Page

Pizza anyone? Students create one of their favorite foods with poster board and construction paper. At the same time they learn the sequence of important events in a plot from the story you assign.

Project Description: Students will create a pizza with each slice showing one important event in the plot. They will then add an illustration to each slice and top their pizza with paper "toppings."

Materials
___tag board
___poster board or construction paper
___white drawing paper for the illustrations
___assorted colors of construction paper for the toppings
___tissue paper (optional)
___scissors, glue

Suggestions:
Green construction paper can be cut for green peppers, white strips of paper can be onions, and brown paper can be turned into pepperoni. Use real pizza boxes to store the plot pizzas. The students can add the title, author, and their names to the outside.

Play
Literature Comes Alive

NAME_____

Your task is to rewrite a short story as a play and present it to the class. Your group will be assigned a short story, tall tale, or fable to read.

Directions:

1. Complete your reading and have a discussion with your group to make sure you understand the story and highlight the important events in the plot.
2. Next, work as a group to rewrite the story into a play to present to the class.
3. Decide which person will play each character and decide on your costumes and stage setting. Construction paper and bulletin board paper can be decorated for your setting.
4. Create your costumes. Use construction paper to make masks and other props. Use your imagination but be sure you are creating costumes that are appropriate for the story you have read.
5. Using time given during class, prepare your scenery and practice your play. Go over your lines and plan out stage actions.
6. Present your play to the class.

Rubric for Literature Comes Alive:

_____works well with others; contributed to the success of the group (10 points)

_____used class time wisely (10 points)

_____came to class prepared with material needed to accomplish task (10 points)

_____costume was appropriate; either made at school or brought accessories from home (10 points)

_____projected voice clearly, loudly, and with expression (10 points)

_____FINAL GRADE/50

Play
Literature Comes Alive

Teacher Page

Students enjoy performing for their peers. They learn presentation skills when they perform a story rewritten as a play, and have fun, too.

Project Description:
Reading is exciting when students are challenged to transform stories into plays that they perform. Each group works together to write the script of a different story or novel. Students receive an individual grade on this project.

Materials:
___costumes and props
___construction paper and/or bulletin
  board paper

___markers, crayons, colored pencils
___tape
___scissors

Suggestions:
• To ensure full participation from each group member, match the number of students in a group with the number of roles available.
• Units that have a theme, such as fables or mythology, work well for this project.
• Depending on how elaborate you want to make it, this project can extend over several days or more for research, script-writing, costume- and scenery-making, and rehearsals.
• When you create groups for this project, make sure that each student will have a role.
• Students can create masks at school, or bring in clothing from home.
• Prepare several comprehension questions for each group to help others understand the plays.
• You can adapt the rubric on the next page to give a grade to each group.
• Students can also create puppets to act out the plays.

Snow White and the Seven Dwarfs

Poem
Plot Poem

NAME_____

Your task is to create a poem that retells the story that you just read. Work cooperatively in small groups and present the poem to the class as a group.

Directions:

1. Each group member will take notes on the important events from that section to be incorporated into the poem. Individual notes will be turned in.
2. After writing down the details, the group should decide on rhyme pattern, then work together to write the poem.
3. Present the poem to the class.
4. Turn in a final copy of the poem including the title and author of the book and the names of each group member. (One grade is given for the entire group, so remember to work cooperatively.)

Rubric for Plot Poem:

_____ notes turned in indicate that each student did his part in note-taking (15 points)

_____ poem covers all important events in the story accurately (15 points)

_____ evidence of a rhyme and rhythm pattern that is consistent (15 points)

_____ poem was written using correct grammar, spelling, punctuation, and capitalization (20 points)

_____ all students in group had a part in the presentation (10 points)

_____ each student read his part pronouncing words correctly (10 points)

_____ each student presenting had eye contact with the audience (10 points)

_____ final copy of poem includes title and author of story and group participants' names (5 points)

_____ FINAL GRADE/100

Poem
Plot Poem

Teacher Page

Poems are a fun way to let your students' creative juices flow. They will learn a new kind of expression and gain valuable presentation skills.

Project Description:
Students work in small groups to retell the major events from a story or novel as a narrative poem. Students present their poems to the class.

Materials:
___paper   ___pencil

Suggestions:
• Review the genre of narrative poetry with students, discussing concepts of rhyme and rhythm and the art of telling a story in verse. Model with some good examples of narrative poems, such as "Casey at the Bat," "The Cremation of Sam McGee," "The Raven," and "The Highwayman."
• Create groups of not more than five members each. Assign one section of a single story read by the class to each person in a group. Make sure each group understands that the events must be presented in order. Alternatively, members of each group could present the events of one story read by that one group.
• Students can represent the characters in the story with costumes or masks.
• Allow one or more class periods for this project.
• Adapt the rubric for this project if you would like to give a grade to each group member.

Other Ideas:
Language Arts - Students can write poems about a particular setting from the story.
• Poems can become songs sung to familiar tunes.

Science - Students can write concept poems on any unit of study, including their science units.

Social Studies - Students can write an ode to a famous person or write poems about a current events topic.

Pop-Ups

NAME_____

Your task is to create a set of three pop-ups on a topic you are studying. Each pop-up will be constructed with a sheet of 8$^{1/2}$" x 11" construction paper or tag board.

Directions:

1. Fold the paper in half from the bottom to the top (so the top edge of the paper meets the bottom edge).
2. Keeping it folded, measure 3" from the right edge of the paper and cut a 2" slit through the folded edge towards the open end.
3. Measure 3" from the left edge of the paper and make another 2" cut towards the open top edge.
4. Unfold your paper so that it sits in an L-shape on your desk. Pop the center piece towards you. You now have a pedestal on which to glue your illustration.
5. Write the name of your topic on the section of the paper that stands up.
6. Glue an illustration of your topic to the popped-out segment.
7. On the bottom section of the paper (that lies flat on your desk), describe the concept that the pop-up illustrates.

Rubric for Pop-Ups:

_____ pop-up one illustrates one concept of your topic; pop-up is labeled with topic title; description is provided to describe what is shown on pop-up; neat/attractive appearance (25 points)

_____ pop-up two illustrates another concept of your topic; pop-up is labeled with topic title; description is provided to describe what is shown on pop-up; neat/attractive appearance (25 points)

_____ pop-up three illustrates a third concept of your topic; pop-up is labeled with topic title; description is provided to describe what is shown on pop-up; neat/attractive appearance (25 points)

_____ correct use of grammar, spelling, punctuation, capitalization, complete sentences (20 points)

_____ your name is on the back of each pop-up (5 points)

_____ FINAL GRADE/100

Pop-Ups

Teacher Page

These homemade pop-ups are reminiscent of the pop-up books your students read as small children. However, they are intended to be displayed already opened. Encourage your students to be creative when they illustrate.

Project Description: After completing a unit of study, students will complete a series of pop-ups that show various concepts of the topic.

Materials:
___tag board or construction paper (three 8 1/2" x 11" squares per student)

___construction paper
___glue

Suggestions:
• Tag board is sturdier and can stand alone when displayed.
• Depending on the unit of study, students might have to spend time in the school library researching their topic. Once their notes are gathered, students will begin to transfer their information onto their pop-ups.

Other Ideas:
Language Arts - Pop-ups can illustrate a series of events in the plot, attributes of a character (such as heroism) or settings from a novel. Students can illustrate and define vocabulary words.

Science - Students can illustrate and describe biomes, food chains, famous scientists, inventions or science safety rules. Students can illustrate science vocabulary.

Social Studies - Students can illustrate and describe Civil Rights laws and leaders, geographical terms, or state/country facts. Students can illustrate social studies vocabulary.

Postcard
Theme Postcard

NAME_____

Your task is to create a postcard that describes to a friend the theme that runs through a short story or novel. Once you have decided upon the theme you are going to develop, you will illustrate it on a large (5" x 7") post card.

Directions:

1. On the front side of the postcard you need to include the title of the story or novel, the name of the story's author, the theme, and an illustration of the theme.
2. On the back of the post card, write a letter to a friend explaining how the theme was developed in the story. Be sure to cite examples from the story.
3. Sign your name at the end of your message.
4. Address the postcard to a friend. You may make up an address.

Rubric for Theme Postcards:

_____ title and author of story are written on the front of the postcard (5 points)

_____ theme is written on the front of the postcard (5 points)

_____ illustration on front of post card relates to the theme in the story (5 points)

_____ message to friend explains the theme and explains how it is relevant to the story (15 points)

_____ your name is signed at the end of the message; address on postcard contains correct elements of an address (5 points)

_____ correct use of grammar: spelling, punctuation, capitalization, complete sentences (15 points)

_____ FINAL GRADE/50

Postcard
Theme Postcard

Teacher Page

Students love getting mail. Postcards, with colorful illustrations on one side and a succinct note on the other, are effective for sharing things you have experienced. Encourage your students to "send" their cards to someone who hasn't read the novel/story.

Project Description: Students will prepare a postcard that discusses the theme of a story or novel.

Materials:
___ 5" x 7" pieces of construction paper or tag board   ___ markers, crayons, colored pencils

Suggestions:
To help assess your students' understanding of theme, hold a class discussion on the various themes in a shared short story or novel and list them on a chart or on the board. Your students will select one theme for their postcard project.

Other Ideas:
Language arts - Students can illustrate several postcards to identify the various settings in a short story or novel.

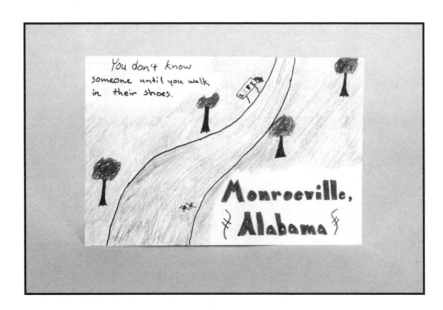

Poster
Missing or Wanted Poster

NAME_____

Pretend that a character from the story or novel you have read is missing. Your task is to create a Wanted poster to help in the hunt for the character.

Directions:

1. Create a likeness of the character you have chosen. If you are artistic, draw a picture. If you have a computer available, you might want to create a computer-generated picture. Another option is to find a picture in a magazine that illustrates your character. If you cannot locate a picture that suits your vision of your character, you can cut the head from one picture and paste it on the body from another picture.
2. Paste your illustration on poster paper under the title "MISSING" or "WANTED".
3. Provide a physical description of the character. For example, you might include how the character was dressed when last seen.
4. Describe the character's habits: places where this character might hang out, cities the character might visit, or places the character might look for employment. You will then want to list possible behaviors the character might exhibit. All of this information is written and pasted on the poster.
5. Include a number to call and a person to contact if the character is seen.
6. On the back of your poster, include the title and author of the story and your name.

Rubric for Missing or Wanted Poster:

_____ poster is titled (5 points)

_____ character illustration is neat/attractive and resembles description in text (5 points)

_____ character's physical attributes are described (5 points)

_____ character's habits are described (5 points)

_____ character's behaviors are described (5 points)

_____ phone number/contact person are provided (5 points)

_____ correct grammar, spelling, punctuation, capitalization (10 points)

_____ project is neat in appearance (5 points)

_____ title and author of story and your name are on back of poster (5 points)

_____ FINAL GRADE/50

Poster
Missing or Wanted Poster

Teacher Page

Wanted posters are a great way to distill the attributes of a character—graphically and in text—into a neat package. Tell your students that, unlike the posters found in post offices and black-and-white Westerns, their versions can be used to find good guys as well as bad guys.

Project Description: After reading a novel or short story, students will create a missing or wanted poster for a character in the story.

Materials:
___construction paper or tag board (approximately 12" x 15")
___magazines
___colored pencils or markers
___glue

Suggestions:
• Have your students pretend that a character from a story or novel they have read is missing or wanted for some reason. The character may have run away, been kidnapped, or simply disappeared.
• Posters can be divided into four sections. Each section can describe a specific concept related to a main topic. Have students include written descriptions and illustrate each section.

Other Ideas:

<u>Language Arts</u> - Posters can be used to describe any of the literary elements of a story or novel. Using a poster, students can display and interpret a poem, provide examples of its figurative language, and provide a biographical sketch of the poet.

<u>Science</u> - Use posters to describe/illustrate characteristics of mammals or to describe and illustrate systems of the human body.

<u>Social Studies</u> - Use the poster format to describe an ancient civilization's location, physical geography, purpose, and culture. Posters also can be made for historical figures, or they can explore the history and purpose of the U.S. Constitution, for example.

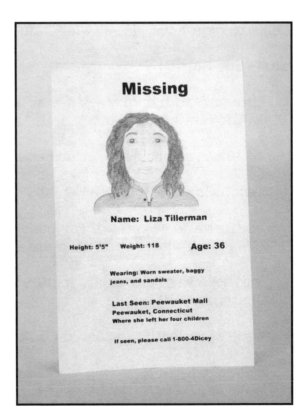

Scroll
Conflict/Resolution Scroll

NAME_____

Thousands of years ago, many books and documents took the form of scrolls, which were rolled sheets of paper. Your modern version will include text on one side and illustrations on the other.

Directions:
1. Choose a conflict/resolution from a story or novel that you have read. (Your teacher may have you choose a problem/solution from a nonfiction source.)
2. Take a 10" x 12" sheet of paper. Leave about 2" at the top of the paper. This will be folded over either a hanger or a wooden dowel.
3. Write the title and author of the story read (or the topic you are describing) at the top of your paper.
4. Divide your paper into two sections. You can divide your paper with a horizontal or diagonal line. Label one section "Conflict" (or "Problem") and describe it as concisely as possible.
5. Label the other section "Resolution" (or "Solution") and describe how the conflict was resolved, (or how the problem was solved.)
6. On the reverse side of your paper, you will again divide the paper into two sections. Label one section "Conflict" (or "Problem") and label the other "Resolution" (or "Solution"). Illustrate the conflict and resolution, (or problem and solution) that you described on the opposite side.
7. Fasten your paper to a hanger or to a wooden dowel.
8. Be sure you have placed your name at the bottom of one of the two sides.

Rubric for Scroll:

_____title and author of story are at the top of the scroll; your name is on one side at the bottom (5 points)

_____conflict (or problem) is labeled and described well (10 points)

_____resolution (or solution) is labeled and described well (10 points)

_____conflict and resolution (or problem and solution) are labeled on illustrated side; well-illustrated (10 points)

_____correct use of grammar, spelling, punctuation, capitalization, complete sentences (10 points)

_____project is neatly presented (5 points)

_____FINAL GRADE/50

Scroll
Conflict/Resolution Scroll

Teacher Page

Scrolls are an ancient but still useful way of conveying information and ideas. These scrolls give your students a fun way to respond to literature.

Project Description: After reading a short story or novel, students must describe and illustrate a conflict and its resolution. (For nonfiction or informational texts, students should identify a problem and its solution.)

Materials:
___bulletin board paper or construction paper
___markers, crayons, colored pencils
___wooden dowels or hangers; glue
___string or yarn (if using the dowels)

Suggestions:
- Bulletin board paper (or butcher paper) that comes on rolls is good to use for this project because it is pliable and easier to handle. (Construction paper will work as well.) A 10" x 12" sheet works best.
- A piece of fabric also makes a good scroll. Students write on paper, cut, and fit it to the fabric.

Other Ideas:

Science - Timeline of the earth's development, planet facts, elements facts, accomplishments of scientists

Social Studies - historical timeliness, contributions of ancient civilizations, countries, state facts and statistics

Language Arts - illustrated plot summary, illustrated character description, illustrated themes with supporting examples, grammar rules with examples, illustrated poetry presentation

Stamps/Coins

NAME_____

Your task is to create a set of three commemorative stamps or coins describing concepts, people, or events in a unit of study. You will decide whether you will prepare stamps or coins.

Directions:

1. You will research concepts, people, or events in your unit of study. Pick three for your stamps or coins.
2. For stamps, you will need three pieces of construction paper approximately 5" square. For coins, you will need three pieces of construction paper approximately 5" round.
3. Label the stamp or coin with the title of your topic. Then you will write one description on each stamp or coin. You will also provide a colorful illustration.
4. Mount them on a piece of poster board or tag board and add a title.
5. Be sure to write your name on the reverse side of the poster.

Rubric for Stamps/Coins:

_____ poster is titled with the topic name: "Commemorative Stamps" or "Commemorative Coins" (5 points)

_____ stamp or coin one is labeled and a well-developed description is provided; stamp is illustrated (20 points)

_____ stamp or coin two is labeled and a well-developed description is provided; stamp is illustrated (20 points)

_____ stamp or coin three is labeled and a well-developed description is provided; stamp is illustrated (20 points)

_____ correct use of grammar, spelling, punctuation, capitalization, complete sentences (20 points)

_____ neat/attractive appearance (10 points)

_____ your name is on the reverse side of the poster (5 points)

_____ FINAL GRADE/100

Stamps/Coins

Teacher Page

Every year, the U.S. government issues commemorative stamps and coins honoring hundreds of people and events. Your students will create their own that apply to a nonfiction topic of study, or which are based on characters in a fictional work.

Project Description: Students will be constructing a set of commemorative stamps or coins reflecting concepts, people, or events in a given topic of study.

Materials:
___ construction paper   ___ markers, crayons, colored pencils
___ tag board or poster board (7" x 18")   ___ glue

Suggestions:
• A class discussion can generate a list of ideas.
• Allow students time to research in the school's media center.

Other Ideas:

Language Arts - use after reading a biography; construct a set for the characters or settings in a novel or short story.

Science - a set for scientists or inventors; mammals, reptiles, birds, insects etc.; planets; bodies of water; types of precipitation.

Social Studies - a set showing different types of maps; a set highlighting events of the Civil Rights Movement or the Depression; famous people of a given time period.

Trading Cards
Plot Trading Cards

NAME_____

Your task is to create a set of trading cards that illustrates six important events in a short story or novel you read.

Directions:

1. Prepare a list of six major events from the story.
2. Develop each idea, including details and characters involved.
3. On one side of each card, write an event. On the opposite side, illustrate this event.
4. Be sure to number your cards in the order the events took place in the story.
5. Once all cards are complete, write the title and author of the story on the front side of an envelope and your name on the reverse side. Place your cards in the envelope.

Rubric for Plot Trading Cards:

_____ envelope shows title and author on the front and your name on the back (5 points)

_____ card one completely describes an event taking place at the beginning of the story; card shows an illustration of the event (10 points)

_____ card two completely describes an event that takes place after the card one event; card shows an illustration of the event (10 points)

_____ card three completely describes an event that takes place after the card two event; card shows an illustration of the event (10 points)

_____ card four completely describes an event that takes place after the card three event; card shows an illustration of the event (10 points)

_____ card five completely describes an event that takes place after the card four event; card shows an illustration of the event (10 points)

_____ card six completely describes an event that takes place after the card five event; card shows an illustration of the event (10 points)

_____ cards are numbered in the order the events occurred (5 points)

_____ descriptions are written using correct grammar, spelling, punctuation, capitalization, complete sentences (20 points)

_____ neat/attractive presentation (10 points)

_____ FINAL GRADE/100

Trading Cards
Plot Trading Cards

Teacher Page

Now you can put your students' love for trading things in class to good use! Apply this time-tested children's hobby to your curriculum with this quick and fun project.

Project Description: After completing a short story or novel, students will prepare a set of trading cards illustrating six important events that took place in the story.

Materials:
____index cards

____colored pencils, markers, crayons
____envelopes (any size will work)

Suggestions:
Another way to present the cards is to string the cards together and display them like a hanging mobile. If displaying this way, have students prepare one card with the title and author of the book on one side and their name on the other side. Students will then punch a hole in the top center and bottom center of each card and fasten the cards together with yarn or string. (The bottom card does not need a hole in the center of the bottom.)

Other Ideas:
Language Arts - Students can make a trading card for each of the five literary elements in the book or story (characterization, setting, plot, theme, conflict/resolution)

Social Studies - trading cards explaining and illustrating the major battles of the Civil War or any other historical event; important historical figures with a brief description of their contributions.

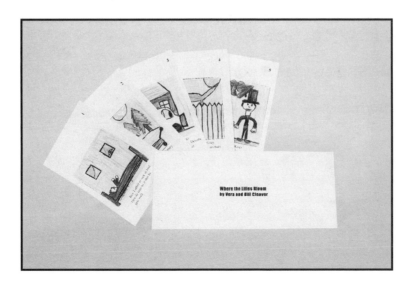

Videotape
Themes Through Taping

NAME_____

Your task is to create a videotape or audiotape discussing a theme in a short story or novel you have read, and show how it relates to the same theme from a movie or television show you have seen or a real-life situation that you have experienced.

Directions:

1. Select one theme and provide three examples of how this theme relates to the story.
2. Then select another piece of literature or a television show, movie, or real life situation where this theme is also evident. Provide at least three examples of how this theme is evident in this selection.
3. Next, prepare a script that you will read during your audio or videotape. Keep your script length to three minutes or less.
4. Mention the title, author, and theme being discussed at the beginning of your tape. Remember to speak clearly and loudly enough to be heard.

Rubric for Themes Through Taping:

_____video begins by naming the title, author, and theme being discussed (5 points)

_____presentation includes examples from the story or novel read that relate to this theme (15 points)

_____presentation includes examples from another literature selection or television, movie, or real life situation where this theme is also evident (15 points)

_____audio: sound is clear; spoken slow enough to understand. video: sound is clear; spoken slow enough to understand; video picture is clear; met the three-minute maximum (10 points)

_____written script is turned in (5 points)

_____FINAL GRADE/50

Videotape
Themes Through Taping

Teacher Page

This project allows students to apply literary concepts to real situations. Because your students explain this concept on camera, you gain a strong, visual tool that gives them specific, constructive feedback.

Project Description:
On videotape, students relate a theme from a short story or novel that relates to real-life situations.

Materials:
___videotape
___video camera
___tripod (if available)
___written script

Suggestions:
• After reading a short story or novel, discuss the themes that run through the story. List them on the board or on a chart. Next, discuss how these themes are also evident in other literature selections as well as in television shows, movies, and in real-life situations.
• Allow students time to practice their presentations with a partner.
• You can adapt this project for audiotape presentation.

Other Ideas:
Language arts - characterization (students can do an on-camera interview); plot (students can act out a scene from the short story or novel)

Website
Literary Website

NAME_____

Your task is to prepare a poster board website showing the plot, setting, characters, conflicts/resolutions, and theme(s) of the novel or short story you have read.

Directions:

1. On a piece of construction paper, title your website www.yourbooktitle.com.
2. The first page you will develop will be titled "Table of Contents" and you will list each literary element (characterization, setting, conflict, resolution, and theme), placing a different colored dot next to each one. Define each term. Illustrate.
3. Next, design a page with the heading www.plot.com Here you will describe the major events that took place in the story. Illustrate.
4. Describe the characters in the story and the page: www.characterization.com. Illustrate.
5. Describe the major settings in the story and title this page www.setting.com. Illustrate.
6. The conflicts/resolutions page, www.conflicts/resolutions.com, will describe the major conflicts and their resolutions. Illustrate.
7. The final page, www.theme.com, will tell the themes that run through the story. Illustrate.
8. On poster board, put the www.yourbooktitle.com heading and your name under it. Paste the table of contents page first with the other pages following. Make sure each page has a colored dot that corresponds to the table of contents.

Rubric for Literary Website:

_____ website is properly titled/your name is under the title (5 points)

_____ table of contents is titled; lists literary terms with definitions; color-coded dots are used for pages that represent each literary element (5 points)

_____ plot page is titled; color-coded; major events of the story are provided; (15 points)

_____ characterization page is titled; color-coded; describes characters; illustrated (15 points)

_____ setting page is titled; color-coded; settings are described; illustrated (15 points)

_____ conflicts/resolutions page is titled; color-coded; major conflicts/resolutions are described; illustrated (15 points)

_____ theme page is titled; color-coded; states theme(s); illustrated (10 points)

_____ correct spelling, usage, punctuation, capitalization, complete sentences (20 points)
_____ FINAL GRADE/100

Website
Literary Website

Teacher Page

Students love surfing the Web for all kinds of information. They're familiar with the "look" of websites and will enjoy creating one of their own.

Project Description: After reading a short story or novel, students will simulate a website on poster board to describe its literary elements of character, setting, plot, theme, conflict, and resolution.

Materials:
___construction paper
___sheet of tag board or poster board
___markers, crayons, colored pencils
___glue

Suggestions:
- This project works well if your students have access to the Internet and are familiar with websites.
- If you can, show your students a few websites online.
- This works well for multicultural-topic projects or literature.

Other Ideas:

<u>Science</u> - parts of a plant, ecosystems, human body systems, compounds, elements

<u>Social Studies</u> - important events or places, different cultures, colonies

The Netherlands Website

Wheel
Conflict/Resolution Wheel

NAME_____

Your task is to create a wheel that describes, in five parts, a conflict and resolution from a short story or novel you have read.

Directions:

1. You will need an 11" x 18" piece of construction paper for the outer cover and a 9-1/4" diameter circle for the wheel to be placed inside the paper.
2. Fold the paper in half, meeting the two shorter edges together.
3. Open the folded piece of paper. Place the circle on top of the bottom half of the piece of paper, in the middle of the sheet. Leave about a1/2" leeway between the fold line and the circle. (When you fold the paper, you will be able to see a part of the circle extend beyond the edge.) If you place the circle directly on the fold, the circle will not turn.
4. Divide the circle into five equal pieces, from the diameter to the edge.
5. Insert the brad through the middle of the circle and out the back of the folded piece of paper. Take out the brad, and keep your finger on the hole.
6. Fold the paper in half over the circle. Insert the brad through all three sheets of paper.
7. Measure 3" from the middle of the top of the folded piece of paper. Cut a 3" x 1" rectangle.
8. Trace the rectangle space on each of the five sections of the circle.
9. Describe the events within one conflict and it resolution, written or typed in five sections. Format the description so that it will fit into the rectangles around the circle. You can either write on the circle or paste your written information onto the circle.
10. Write the title and author of the story of novel you read on the outside cover.
11. Illustrate the cover.
12. Place your name on the back of the project cover.

Rubric for Conflict/Resolution Wheel:

_____ cover shows title and author; illustrated (5 points)

_____ segment 1 describes how this conflict began (15 points)

_____ segment 2 describes the conflict unfolding (15 points)

_____ segment 3 continues with the conflict as it begins to be resolved (15 points)

_____ segment 4 continues with conflict as it is being resolved (15 points)

_____ segment 5 clearly states the resolution (15 points)

_____ correct use of grammar, punctuation, spelling, capitalization, complete sentences (15 points)

_____ neat, attractive presentation; your name on the back of the project (5 points)

_____ FINAL GRADE/100

Wheel
Conflict/Resolution Wheel

Teacher Page

Students love to create this moving representation of an abstract concept.

Project Description: Students create a moving wheel that is placed within a folded piece of paper which has a small opening cut out from it. Students write on the wheel and view the conflict and its resolution through the opening. This project is ideal for the kinesthetic learners in your class.

Materials:
___ 2 sheets of 11" x 18" construction paper per student
___ fastening brads (1 per student)
___ markers, crayons, colored pencils
___ scissors
___ rulers

Suggestions:
- Prepare several 9-1/4"-diameter wheel templates for students to use as tracing masters.
- Before students begin this project, they should understand how to identify a conflict and resolution from a piece they have read. Ask students to draft a description of this conflict and its resolution, dividing the information into five small segments that will later be placed on the wheel.
- Model this project first, so students understand how to properly position the wheel inside the folded piece of construction and attach the brad so that the wheel turns.

Other Ideas:

Science - planets, diseases, accomplishments of scientists, inventors, facts about vertebrates or invertebrates

Social Studies - ancient civilization achievements, facts about continents, geography definitions and terms, facts about presidents, accomplishments of explorers

Rubric Subject Index

About the Author

As a middle-school language arts teacher for over 30 years, Jane Ferber's innovative approach to language-arts instruction has earned her several awards, including the Gladys Prior Award for Teaching Excellence in 2002 and the 2003 Teacher of the Year for the Florida Council of Teachers of English. She is a National Board Certified Teacher in the area of Early Adolescent English/Language Arts. She earned a Master's in Reading from the University of North Florida.

Jane lives in Jacksonville, Florida and enjoys teaching, volunteering with a mental health association in her community, and spending time with her son, Adam, who attends the University of Florida.

Since 1997, she has traveled across the U.S. providing workshops and presenting at conferences for middle-school language-arts teachers.

For more information about her workshops and presentations, please contact Maupin House at 800-524-0634 or visit www.maupinhouse.com. You can also write to Jane directly at janefeber@hotmail.com.